SMITH
OF LAMBETH

To Frank,
the Rockstar!

SMITH
OF LAMBETH

And Other Tales: A Memoir

DAVID JONES

More a beggar
than a
May 2022 King

FCP

Full Court Press
Englewood Cliffs, New Jersey

First Edition

Copyright © 2019 by David Jones

Published in the United States of America
by Full Court Press, 601 Palisade Avenue
Englewood Cliffs, NJ 07632
fullcourtpress.com

ISBN 978-1-946989-27-7
Library of Congress Catalog No. 2019930383

Editing and book design by Barry Sheinkopf

Cover image by Jacquelyn Ashley

The "About the Author" photo on p. 195, by Bob
Schellhammer, originally appeared in the Vineyard Gazette.

"Not vernal showers to budding flowers
Not autumn to the farmer
So dear can be as thou to me
My fair, and lovely charmer."

—Robert Burns, 1759–1796,
from "Westlin Winds"

TABLE OF CONTENTS

————————

To Begin, 1

One of Ours, 7

The Blackberry-and-Apple Pie, 47

Bibbicot Kim and Her Morning Tea, 52

The Unfortunate Jones, or Death at the Final, 58

Thomas Grey and Mr. Legget, 67

Two Swimming Disasters, 78

Smith of Lambeth, 87

My Friend Sydney, 96

Not Forgotten, 103

A Chance Encounter, 114

The Mountain and the Sergeant, 123

Notes on Life in Uganda, 141

Ronnie Mansfield and the Incompetent Mister, 150

An Embarrassing Spelling Mistake, and The Mighty Atom, 157

The Program Seller and Queen Salote, 166

Lenny, Frank, and Hildegarde, 175

The Sad Demise of the Peckham Health Center, 183

Greenwich Park, and the Strange Sign in the Pond, 187

Where We Are Now: Endings, 192

About the Author, 195

TO BEGIN

S MITH OF LAMBETH LOOKED THE PART but was more embellishment than substance. The saga of my schoolboy battle with Smith was the first story I wrote down, and it is still a favorite: To keep myself off the streets and out of the pubs, I decided to write down other memories too, ranging from experiences in England during World War II to being a music hall singer in New York City in the 1980s. (I came from London to the USA in 1965, with the intent of staying for six months or so; more than fifty years later, I am still here).

I began with my evacuation experience in World War II. It took a lot of time to put that story together, and some research. In 2005, I visited the Leicestershire village of Swinford, where I had spent the majority of my time as an evacuee. My wife Louise was with me, and I took her to see the centerpiece of the village, the splendid twelfth-century Norman church. After I had shown her where I sat in the choir stalls as a very mediocre boy soprano, I wrote a message in the church visitors' book. I mentioned my time as an evacuee in Swinford, and that I'd sung in the church choir. I left my American address and an English phone number.

Some time later, I received two letters—one from the verger of the church, the other from the current owner of the house where I had lived with the Hornsby family. Both letters invited me to visit.

Then, while in England, I received a phone call. The voice on the other end said, "This is Mary Barnett." Mary was the sister of Roland, my best friend during those war years, and also a friend of Jean Hornsby, with whom we both went to school.

I was bowled over, and it led to me going back to the village, with Louise, to meet Mary, Roland, and Jean. They had all aged gracefully and were happy and in excellent health. It was a most wonderful visit; we had a splendid pub lunch and talked for a long time, recalling those wartime years. They had not felt the need, or the desire, to live anywhere else but Leicestershire. Mary still lived in Swinford; Roland and Jean were no more than three miles away.

Mary was a goldmine of memories and information—she knew a great deal about village history and what had happened to the friends we had during the war. She set me straight on many things and corroborated my memories of others. She also reminded me of details of village life and of the role the Women's Institute took in caring for evacuees.

I went to the Imperial War Museum in London, to remind myself of what the air raid shelters looked like. The Anderson Shelter was so small that all I could think of was, How on earth had six, and sometimes seven, people managed to fit in it?

Speaking about that experience set in motion other memories, especially of schooldays right after the war. Swimming races, boxing matches, art classes, teachers who had a positive influence—and those who did not—all seemed fodder for a tale.

Later, I turned to work-related memories, starting with my first job after leaving school, which led to the story "The Chance Encounter" and to my time working and living in East Africa.

I thought that my royal duties at the coronation of Queen Elizabeth II would surely lead *somewhere*, but maybe it takes more than selling programs to be noticed. However, I do hope that you enjoy reading about the magnificent Queen Salote of Tonga, and that wet and windy day chosen for the coronation.

Memory sometimes tells me that my sojourn in East Africa was all excitement and filled with adventure. It must have had some dull and humdrum times and some disappointing ones too, but I did get to sit one empty bar stool away from the great Louis Armstrong, climb Mount Kilimanjaro, and walk on the beautiful white sands of Mombasa. So it had its charms.

I was surprised by how difficult some of the memories were. The most difficult came in writing "Robbed." The memory of being so unjustly disqualified by an unpleasant school teacher in that London championship swimming race was overwhelming.

Family stories led me to research my father's Welsh family, which resulted in the telling of the sad tale of my great-uncle Will Jones. He came to his unfortunate end nearly a hundred and twenty years ago while scoring the winning goal in a football cup final. I went, with Louise, to the Isle of Wight to find Great-Uncle Will's grave, and to learn details of his story, which I tell in "The Unfortunate Jones." As I read the coroner's report and newspaper articles from 1899, I think I came to some extent to know who my great-uncle was.

I took a trip across the channel to a First World War Cemetery in Dickebusch, Belgium, and found the grave of Great-Uncle Reuben Skeels. He was killed in action in 1917. In the Second World War, my family lost William (Bibbo) Stubbs. He went down while on a bombing mission and is remembered with honor on a monument in

Runnymead. Laying a hand on stone memorials of family members you never knew does, in some way, bring them a little closer, and you do feel a bond.

An important part of my life has been as a singer of traditional folksong and of Victorian-era music hall songs. I have made a number of recordings, solo and with various groups, including one with the guitarist Bill Shute that was aimed at young audiences. It was called *Widdecombe Fair* and received a Parents Choice Gold Award. Occasionally, I get to hear myself on the radio, which sometimes is fun but often is not. The big reward of performing has been the great people and brilliant musicians I have met over the years. I have had good times, interspersed with disappointments and, sometimes, failure. Failure in performance is usually self-inflicted, mostly due to lack of preparation.

I have had some minor success in theater and have been well reviewed. One reviewer said, "David Jones is a lusty old goat." How can you beat that? I enjoyed being in plays by the great Norwegian Henrik Ibsen. He has become one of my favorite playwrights. Being a spear carrier at the Metropolitan Opera and a sometime member of the New York Gilbert and Sullivan Players were also great experiences. However, the guts of my income has always been through my training as a structural engineer, and I have never had difficulties in getting a job in that profession, which also gave great opportunities to travel.

I don't think there is anything extraordinary about these stories, or my experiences. All of my old mates in South East London have similar tales of relatives involved in the World Wars and can recount good and bad experiences at school.

Writing these tales has been interesting, although a little taxing to my aged brain, and has only been partially successful in keeping me off the streets and out of the pubs. They have, however, revived some wonderful memories. Standing at the top of Mount Kilimanjaro, the roof of Africa, on that glorious and golden morning, was an experience I will never forget.

I could go on, but I think that's enough for a beginning, so (with some trepidation) I offer my stories.

ONE OF OURS

The World War II Evacuation From London, 1939

MEMORY IS FALLIBLE—especially when we try to recall what happened to us when we were very young. In later years, we talk to parents, aunts and uncles, and other folks who were around at the time, and try to establish a consensus about what happened. The evacuation of school children from London in World War II has been widely covered. Stories from children, parents, and families who took in evacuees have been collected and made available in books and films. This is what I remember, although I am sure there are some errors.

Some Background: Pre-War Life

In the mid-1930s, my parents, Richard William and Ethel Caroline Jones (née Draper), along with my older brother, Richard Charles, and I, left our rented house in an East London area known as The Isle of Dogs, the heart of London's docklands. The Island, as it is commonly referred to, is on the north bank of the river Thames. We moved across the river to its south side. In local parlance, we moved to "the other side of the water."

There is no definitive explanation for the name "The Isle of Dogs"; it may have been where King Henry VIII kept his hunting dogs, or it maybe a corruption of "The Isle of Ducks", no-one knows. A long time ago, it was marshland which, over the centuries got drained and developed. On its east, west, and south sides, it is bordered by the River Thames, where it makes a great meander. The West India Docks were opened sometime around 1800, cutting across the north side of the loop, effectively creating an island, but it had been referred to as an island long before then. I don't know why.

I would have been one, maybe two, years old at the time, and I don't know why we left. I have no personal memories of the Island, but my family's folklore, such as it is, is rooted in stories of island life, and of Millwall Football Club. In the 1890s and 1900s, my paternal grandfather and two of his brothers played for Millwall. My grandfather also played for Wales. So for better or worse, Millwall is my family football club. I heard stories about "The Mudchute," which in its beginnings consisted of excavated material from the building of the docks, and of an enormous fellow known as Tiny Joyce. He was Millwall's goalkeeper in the early days of the club and, we were told, a legendary figure. My aunts and uncles told stories of two local boxers, Ernie Jarvis, a very good flyweight, and Teddy Baldock. Teddy, known as the "Pride of Poplar," at one time held a version of the world bantamweight title.

Stories of my maternal grandfather, Charlie Draper, were intriguing. He was an itinerant dockworker, concertina player, heavy drinker, and singer of sentimental songs. There are photographs of him in his World War 1 soldier's suit, but I doubt he saw any military action. He and my grandmother didn't live past their mid-forties, so

I never knew them. When they died, they left seven children, four girls, Lily, Ethel, Edie and Nellie, and three boys, Charley, Ernie, and Arthur. They ranged in age from infants to a nineteen-year-old; that was my aunt Lily. The story is that social workers came round to the family house to take the two or three youngest children away and put them in foster homes, but Aunt Lily refused to let them go. "We are sticking together" she told the social workers. I once asked her how she managed. She said it was with the help of good neighbors. I believe that my Aunt Lily was a hero. To add to the long list of aunts and uncles, Dad had two younger siblings, Bill, and Ada. My parents and all these aunts and uncles were born on the island in the early part of the twentieth century. They grew up, went to school, got jobs, married, and lived in the hardscrabble neighborhood of the Docklands. They were true East Enders.

Gradually, members of my family, aunts, uncles, cousins and grandparents, drifted away from the island and crossed the river to live in and around Greenwich and Blackheath. My parents took us a couple of miles further west, to Rural Place, a very small cul-de-sac, in New Cross, South East London. Rural Place opened onto Queens Road, a heavily trafficked thoroughfare that runs into the famous Old Kent Road.

I have very few detailed memories of Rural Place, but I know that there were terraced two-story brick houses on one side of the street, and a wall on the other. What was behind the wall, I don't know. All the houses had outdoor toilets and tiny back and front gardens. Most of my memories of that time are too blurred to try to write down, but I do remember having a children's pedal car that I could "drive" up and down the street. Another isolated memory is seeing the old-fashioned gaslights being replaced by spanking new electric ones. The days of the Gas Lamp Lighter Man, who used to manually turn on the lights, were over.

Just around the corner from Rural Place, on Queens Road, was a row of small shops, Long's Butchers, which sold traditional cuts of meat, along with traditional savory dishes like Pease Pudding, made from yellow split peas, and a fried chopped-meat dish called Faggots. Pop's Sweet Shop was a favorite place for children, and there was a very good bakery. Waller Road Elementary School was a couple of blocks away, and there were good bus and tramcar services to all parts of London.

The tramcars are now long gone; they were noisy, and the embedded steel tracks were a nightmare for cyclists. A nasty spill was certain when a tire got caught in the tracks. A fire station was nearby, close to New Cross Gate. The fire engines were an exciting attraction to young boys and girls.

Our playground was generally the street, but London has so many wonderful open spaces, and just a short bus ride from Rural Place we could find Greenwich Park, and the "dark colored heath" known as Blackheath. The park and the heath gave us four hundred beautiful acres for recreation. We also took family trips, with aunts and uncles, down to a coastal town in Kent called St. Mary's Bay. A couple of uncles had cars, in which we traveled to what became affectionately known in my family as "The Bay," all my memories of which are idyllic. The sun was always shining and the sea water was always warm.

So much for memory.

All in all, New Cross was safe and convenient, a fine place to live in and raise a family. Milk was delivered to the doorstep, a rag-and-bone man came around with his horse-drawn cart to take anything that was being thrown out, and weekly rents were paid in cash.

We were living in that gritty working-class neighborhood on September 3, 1939, at the outbreak of the Second World War.

I was much too young to have any awareness of the tensions that must have been brewing among the grownups over news of a possible war with Germany. It was just twenty-one years after the end of World War I, the war that the politicians said would put an end to all wars. So grown-ups had very clear memories of that terrible conflict, and were fearful. My family had lost my Dad's relative, Rueben Skeels in that terrible conflict; he fell in 1917 and is buried in Belgium.

Hundreds of thousands of military veterans, many still suffering from wounds and traumas inflicted in the war, were still relatively young men. Now, it seemed, it was all about to happen again. The German Army marched into Poland on September 1, the prime minister, Neville Chamberlain, spoke to the nation over the wireless on September 3, announcing that Great Britain was now in a state of war with Germany, and that was it: World War II was on.

The Evacuation

Since 1933, when Adolf Hitler became the German chancellor, members of the British Government had been aware that the likelihood of war with Germany was great. Along with many other arrangements they made in the event war did come were plans to evacuate schoolchildren from likely danger zones to the safety of the countryside. They had to be moved out of areas that were likely to be bombed, and into safe ones. Teachers, mothers with very young children, and other vulnerable folk were to be included in the evacuation.

Executing those plans involved the relocation of 3.5 million people, young and old—a gigantic operation. Plans for "Operation Pied Piper," as it was called, had been going on for some time, and many experts had worked long and hard on the logistics of how to move so many, in a short space of time, to a safe place.

In some instances, they did not thoroughly consider what would be the wisest places. Thousands of London schoolchildren were sent to the south coast of England—not the best of ideas since, once the German army occupied France, it was just twenty-one miles away from the English coast at the shortest crossing of the channel. Within less than a year, all those children would have to be moved again.

Before the great exodus from London, everyone in the cities, young and old, was given a gas mask, carried in a cardboard box and hung around the neck with a piece of string. The very youngest children received Mickey Mouse gas masks, so they would want to put them on. Fortunately, the need to wear the masks never arose.

After several trials and dummy runs, when children took their backpacks and gas masks to school and then brought them home again, the great day, or days, arrived (the operation was actually spread over four days, September 1 to 4), but everyone knew it was coming. Parents took their children to the school yard with their luggage and with large name labels pinned to their jackets. Then they went to the railway station to see their children off and say goodbye. I don't know where my group departed from, but it was probably Victoria station.

I have a cloudy memory of the chaos when we were all put on the train. The older children were shouting, laughing, and fighting. I do believe that my mother and my dear aunt Lily were on the platform trying to catch sight of me and my brother. At still a few days short of my 5th birthday, I had no idea of what was going on. I think I was totally bewildered, and maybe afraid; after all, we were being taken away from our parents.

The train quickly completed the fifty-mile journey to the south coast. Many of the children had never left their own districts in London, so this was their first real journey away from home—and the first time many of them would see the sea. The experience of country life would be a culture shock for them. It would also be a shock for the families that took them into their homes. I have no memory of the train journey, and I am not sure of the name of the town we were taken to either. I think it was Portslade. It was close to the South Downs and to Brighton.

On arrival, we were all taken to a community center where a nurse checked us out for common ailments. Then the boys were sat on the floor on one side of the hall, and the girls on the other side. There were social workers sitting at some tables at the front of the hall, facing us.

Then local people came in to choose children and take them home. When one was selected, some formalities with the social workers followed; then, off they went. The people adopting the children were good souls but selective in their choices. And who could blame them? Some of the evacuees came from very poor families, and from districts in London where life was very hard. They were, on the outside, tough kids, and a lot of them did not get chosen. A child from the East End of London was almost an alien creature to the folks of Sussex. I was with my brother and determined not to get separated; since most people didn't want to take in two children, we were still there at the end of the day.

At one point, I was chosen by a family who had a child of my age, and we were walking out through the door when, realizing that my brother was not with me, I panicked. I remember the mother saying, "Don't you want to come and play with Michael?" Well, it seems I didn't, and I ran back to where my brother was sitting. So at the end of the day, we, along with some other boys and girls, did not get foster parents.

We were all housed somewhere for the night. My memory—of all the boys being in one enormous bed, and all the girls in another—is probably distorted. An associated memory of the boys having fun shouting out that there was a "Jerry" under the bed may be true (the term denoted both a German and a chamber pot—it was a running joke).

The next morning, social workers took us leftover children around town to find homes for us. The social worker who took my brother and me was not in the mood for discussions or negotiations. She knocked on a door and, when it was opened by a middle-aged woman, she pushed us forward, telling the poor woman, in no uncertain terms, that she had two evacuees from London to look after.

The woman said she didn't want any evacuees, but she was outgunned.

She and her husband were nice people but unequipped to handle two boys, five and nine, from London, though they did as best they could. They took us up into the South Downs to see the Devil's Dyke, which is said to be the Devil's foot print. I had no doubt that that is what it was, and I still don't. They told us that the next footprint was somewhere in Spain—quite a stride. I didn't know where Spain was, but it sounded far away, (at the age of five, I could not imagine how far).

We were only with this couple for a few weeks and then moved on to a series of short-term billets. One stop was with a young couple; the woman was expecting a baby, and her husband had a motor bike. He took us for rides on the back of that bike. I made a point of showing them my toothbrush and demonstrating that I knew how to brush my teeth. The rest is a blank.

After these temporary situations, we were placed in more permanent housing in the famous seaside town of Brighton, known for its pier, pebbled beach, and Regency-period buildings. We were to live with a Baptist family—Mr. and Mrs. Cole, an older couple with two unmarried daughters, in their terraced house (i.e., row house) in a pleasant part of the city.

We stayed mostly in the back of the house with the daughters, who looked after us and made sure that we said our prayers. They got us ready for school and so on, and prepared our meals, which we ate with them. There were usually some treats on the table, but whether we got them or not depended on how the daughters judged our table manners. If they decided those had not been good enough, then no treats. We had to ask to be excused from the table in French— "*Pardonnez-moi, si'l vous plait*," I think was the phrase. There were a few other things we had to say in French, like *bon soir*, but I forget what they were.

Serious disciplinary matters were handled by Mr. Cole, but there weren't too many of those. We were never physically punished; our reprimands occurred more in the form of lectures or having to read or write something. At the time, I couldn't read or write, so I probably just got lectures.

I was also chastised for bed wetting. The sisters would call me up to the bedroom to show me the wet sheets. Well, nothing much

I could do about that.

Mr. Cole was a Baptist lay preacher, and we were only allowed into his part of the house on rare occasions. Christmas Day 1939 was one of them. We all ate Christmas dinner in his private room. I was in awe of being allowed into a place that was so very secret. The mouth-watering Christmas pudding was the highlight, with thick yellow custard poured over it and small silver three-penny pieces stuffed into it. Many of the silver coins were accidentally swallowed, but it was good luck if you did find one. I can't recall much in particular about that dinner, but we got presents, and we wore the paper hats that flew out from the Christmas crackers when we pulled them. Everybody in Britain pulled Christmas crackers and wore paper hats on Christmas Day. I'd bet that even King George wore a paper hat.

We went to regular school during the week, and to Sunday school; My memory of these schools is too blurred to try to write anything about them. At the Cole's house, we learned to knit—plain and pearl.

There was thus an order to living with the Cole family; but the situation did not last long. Mrs. Cole became ill, and we had to move on. Once it had been determined where our next billets would be, the Coles and their daughters tried to explain why we had to move, and showed us on a map where we were going. The latter meant nothing to me. We were bound for Hove, which is just west of Brighton. I was quite upset with the move for, though the Coles' was a very strict household, it was secure.

Hove is a fine town, and its relationship to the sea is the same as Brighton's. We soon realized that we were very lucky. We were taken in by Mr. and Mrs. Bishop, who welcomed us with open arms.

He was a car mechanic, and he and his wife had no children—at least there were none living in the house when my brother and I were there. Like the Coles, they lived in a terraced house, but there was a large attached garage where Mr. Bishop did his work.

They were kind people, maybe in their late thirties to early forties. We must have changed schools, but I have no memory of that. The Bishops kept two birds, a canary and a budgerigar (called a parakeet in America); the birds delighted us, and from time to time Mr. Bishop allowed them to fly around the room and sit on the tops of their cages. He sometimes took us out for car rides as well, which was always an exciting experience. They were warm people, and ours seemed an ideal situation. We liked being in their house, and they wanted us there.

But the government in London had finally realized by then that having so many children living on the south coast was a bad idea. The stony beaches were mined, and barbed wire had been strung along the sea walls to keep people off them. Although the coast of France could not be seen from Brighton, farther to the east, around Dover, the beaches of Normandy were only twenty miles away and clearly defined. With powerful telescopes it was possible to see the Germans on those beaches—and they could see us. It had been across that stretch of water that William, Duke of Normandy, sailed his boats to invade England in 1066. There was real fear that the German army would try to do the same.

To this point, 1940 had been a very quiet year on the domestic front, so much so that it became known as the "Phony War." Nevertheless, an order came to relocate the remaining children away from the coast and send them to safer locations in the British Isles and, in some cases, Canada and the U.S.A. Having to move, and leave the Bishops, was very stressful on us and affected my brother deeply. The Bishops sat us down and explained what was about to happen—that the government had ordered all of us evacuees to be moved away from the south coast, and we had to follow the order. They did not want to see us go, they said, but they had no say in the matter. My brother has always been far more stoic than I, but that moment was too much for him. The Bishops comforted him as best as they could.

A few days later, we said a tearful goodbye to the Bishops and went on our way—back to London for a while.

I have often wished that I'd kept in touch with Mr. and Mrs. Bishop, and visited them before they died. They were very special people. Maybe not enough has been written about the folks who took in child evacuees and made them part of their families. Many grew attached to the children in their care, and the parting must have been difficult.

The Move to Swinford and School Life

Many families with children had drifted back to London during the period of the Phony War that ended in June 1940, and although there were signs of military preparations all around, London seemed safe enough and life there went on as usual. Then came Dunkirk, the Battle of Britain, and the Blitz; 1940 marked a decisive turning point and became a make-or-break year for Britain.

I am not sure precisely when, but at some time in 1940 my brother and I were moved to the market town of Lutterworth, in Leicestershire, which is in the English Midlands. We lived with a grocer's family named Drake, but were only there for a month or so.

Then we moved all of three miles to the village of Swinford, a farming community with a population of three or four hundred. It had originated as a Saxon settlement, Suin Heaford, first recorded in the *Domesday Book* in 1086.

The village had a two-room schoolhouse, a woman's institute, two pubs, a chapel, and a splendid twelfth-century church. There were also two small shops, one of which included a post office, and then there was Mr. Groom, the blacksmith. It was fun to watch him

All Saints Church, Swinford

at work at his furnace, the sparks flying as he hammered out the horseshoes on his anvil, and then nailed them to the horses' hooves. Swinford had one policeman, named Bruin. He had a car, one of two or three in the village. There was also a squire—well, I'm not sure if he was a *real* Squire, I don't even know what the qualifications to be a squire are, but he was the most important resident in all of Swinford. Or maybe he just thought he was. He lived in a large house on his farm, and invariably rode on horseback through the village. When the Leicestershire hunt gathered outside one of the village pubs before riding off with their yelping hounds to chase foxes, there was the squire in his bright red hunting jacket with shiny buttons. The laboring folk and the young people in the village, followed the hunt on foot.

The village also boasted a private bus service, Gee's Busses. Mr. Gee, who always wore a snazzy cap, provided his service to Swinford folks, and to people in neighboring villages. His longest journey was to the town of Rugby, all of six miles away. There was another bus service, the Midland Reds, that offered longer rides than Mr. Gee did, but they were dilapidated old vehicles and were always breaking down.

About twenty or so London evacuees who preceded my brother and me to the village had overwhelmed the village school. They had come with their teacher, Miss Lindsey, in the first wave of evacuees at the outbreak of the war. Miss Lindsey was said to be a breath of fresh air in the village. She made learning fun and is remembered by older villagers to this day. I think she had moved on by the time I started at the school. Evacuees arrived with a ration book, a gas mask, and some with no more than the clothes on their backs. Most of the housing for the evacuees was arranged through the woman's institute. The way the villagers remember it, it was, in general, the less well-off who cared for the children in their small cottages, not so much the better-off folks in their large houses. The cockney accent of the evacuees was a source of amusement and bewilderment for the villagers; likewise, the strong Leicestershire accent, and some of the customs, had the evacuees making fun of their "country cousins."

My brother and I lived in a fine house with the Hornsbys and their two daughters. My mother also spent some time living in the Hornsby house, though I can't remember for how long. The house had a really large backyard where Mr. Hornsby kept hens, ducks, and pigs. The pigs were bred to have piglets, which when they got to be nice and plump were sold. One day, the pig herself would be sold. When the local butcher came for Mama Pig, she just knew that something very bad was in store for her. She ran around the yard in a panic, and her squeals of fright tore at us children, but the butcher caught up with her. He put his pistol to her head and shot her. She fell like a stone. It was a startling lesson in country life for a child from London. "A time to kill, and a time to heal," says the book of Ecclesiastes.

Beyond the backyard lay a large, splendid orchard. All the fruits of England grew there—apples, plums, pears, and damsons in the trees, red and black currents, gooseberries, and blackberries blossomed in their own seasons on well-tended bushes. There was also a swing hanging from the branch of an apple tree that was enjoyed by children and grownups alike. Like all the other houses in the village, it had neither running water nor flush toilets, but it did have a pump, and rain barrels were set under the downspouts around the buildings, so the water was good.

The eldest of the Hornsby girls was Jean, a very fast runner who would always beat me in the race home from school. There were two other evacuees in the house, sisters from London. The older always did her best to please, while the younger was as tough as nails and did not care what anyone thought of her. She was a big problem for the teachers at the village school. The older girl helped with

Aunt Nellie and me with Mr. Hornsby's dog.
Photo taken in the large farmyard on the Hornsby
property. Aunt Nellie was visiting from London.

chores around the house. While doing some cleaning, she was told to use some elbow grease. She became very upset, and said, "I don't have no money to buy elbow grease!"

Mr. Hornsby had a lovely but untrained sheepdog. I have a memory of a local farmer coming to the house to complain that the dog had been worrying his sheep, a serious complaint in a farming community. Not all dogs belonging to herding breeds can be successfully trained, so something had to be done. What the outcome was for this beautiful dog, I don't know. Hopefully, she found a safe harbor far away from farms and bleating sheep.

All of the children in the house went to the two-room village school, where we spent most of our time making hooked rugs and raffia place mats. What became of those rugs, I don't know; maybe the teachers had a cottage industry going. I started in the class for children aged five to eight; my brother, Richard, was in the class for eight- to eleven-year-olds. The younger children were taught by Miss Burgess, a somewhat rotund woman who traveled to the school from a neighboring village on a very large motorbike. Mrs. Mechim, a sharp-featured and very severe woman, taught the older children. Apart from the hooked rugs, we made attempts to learn cursive writing and how to add and subtract. We were given bulbs to grow lilies for Easter, which we took to church on Easter Sunday. We also grew radishes (I'm not sure why). The vicar, the Reverend Taylor, came to the school now and then to give us some religious education. He had spent some time in South Africa, and he tried to teach us how to say the Lord's Prayer in Afrikaans. It didn't work out too well.

It was a very good deal to be a vicar. A fine house, called a manse, went with the job, along with a housekeeper. Sometime later, the Reverend drafted me into the church choir, not, I think, for my singing voice, but because by that time I was one of the few children of my age who could read. Once in a while, the Nature Man would turn up at the school to show us his collection of birds' eggs, and to tell us how to look after the countryside. I liked his visits. Then there was the visiting nurse, who came to check us out for head lice, a not-uncommon condition at the time.

As well as my brother, and I, the two sisters from the Hornsby house, several other evacuees from London, and some from Coventry, attended the school. A number came from very hard and deprived backgrounds, and they were constantly fighting. One day, I saw one of the boys, a kid named Ernie, crying. He told me that his father had been killed on some railroad tracks in London—he'd gotten into an altercation with Ernie's much older brother, and it ended up on the tracks. I don't know how it happened, but the episode taught me that even tough kids could be hurt and shed tears.

The London children did get up to mischief in the village, but they were sometimes blamed for things that they did not do. A farmer came to the Hornsby house once to accuse my brother of blocking one of his streams. It was pointed out to the farmer that my brother had been with his school in Devon for several months. We also heard people say that "this was a nice village before the Londoners came." But most of the villagers were very kind and tried hard to help the evacuees assimilate. There was a trick that village children played on the Londoners: They'd take unsuspecting evacuees up to a hedgerow to show them the nest of a "push-ditch bird." When the young evacuee leaned forward to see the nest, they were pushed into the drainage ditch that ran alongside of the hedgerows.

My best friend in the village was Roland Barnett, a farmer's son. In the summer months I went with him, and sometimes his sister Mary, to the fields for haymaking and harvesting. I think that I imagined that we were of great help to Mr. Barnett, the farmer, but we were probably more in the way than anything else. Mrs. Barnett brought sandwiches for us, which we would eat at mid-day, sitting on the grass and watching out for angry wasps. Once, Roland took a large bite of his sandwich that happened to be covered with wasps. I forget what the upshot was, but it wasn't pleasant for Roland. In my memory, all those days of the haymaking and harvest were filled with warmth and glorious sunshine, but I know that my memory must be faulty. It was, after all, English weather, and there must have been many wet and windy days.

I enjoyed seeing the great shire horses pull the carts, and the mighty threshing machine at work as it knocked the grain off the stalks. Rats ran out from the sheaves and hayricks, chased by excited dogs. It was a wonderful experience. In these busy seasons, the small farmers helped each other out with labor and the machines that were moved from farm to farm. Building the hayricks involved so much work: The hay had to be kept dry so it wouldn't rot because it was needed to feed the animals in the winter. This was tough to do in rainy England, but it had to be done. The ricks were covered with tarpaulins held down by ropes tied to stakes driven into the ground.

When the day's work was over, the men and women would head for home. Some walked and others rode bikes, but the farmer had to get the horses back to the stables. He sat on his horse sideways, his long legs hanging down one side of the animal. Wearing a cloth cap and stiff leather gaiters below the knees, he rolled and smoked a cigarette as the horses plodded home. No one had to direct the horses—they knew where to go, down to their own stalls in the barn. I remember sitting on one of those great horses for the ride home. I sat right up at the neck and hung onto the mane. It was the only part of the horse where my legs would fit. A late nineteenth-century English poet named Cicely Fox Smith wrote many fine poems about farming and seafaring life, including a most beautiful one about the young men and the horses of the First World War called "Homeward." The poem paints a picture of a soldier, looking back, after his experiences of warfare in the trenches and seeing the carnage among the men and the horses, to the peaceful days before the war started in 1914; she describes the men riding home from the fields in the evening twilight, and sitting sideways:

Dead lads and shadowy horses, I see them all the same,
I see them and I know them and I call them each by name,
Riding down from harvest, with all the west aglow
And the lads all sitting sideways and singing as they go.

I sing this poem to a beautiful musical setting by the late Sarah Morgan, and when I sing it I think of those days when I was going home from the fields in Swinford, with the farmer sitting sideways on his horse.

Many of the farmers employed ladies from the Woman's Land Army. These women wore smart uniforms and replaced the men who had been called up for military service. Some of the women came from towns and were not familiar with farm work, so to be of use to the farmer, they had to have training. They worked hard and did the best they could to help with the war effort and, to my recollection, were a cheerful bunch.

Three times a year the village church had full attendance— at Christmas and Easter, and for the service to celebrate the harvest, at which the area around the altar would be piled high with seasonal produce from the fields. Beautiful loaves of bread, decorated with patterns of wheat, were arranged among the produce to make a glorious display. Maybe time has exaggerated that memory—childhood memories are not always reliable—but I do know that some of the best hymns were sung at the harvest service. "Bringing in the Sheaves" and "Sing the Song of Harvest Home" were favorites. No need to be timid; you could just belt out those glorious hymns. "All is safely gathered in, ere the winter storms begin." A number of these were set to traditional folk tunes, especially those used for drinking songs. A drinking song set to the tune used for the harvest hymn "All Good Gifts Around Us," for example, is:

Put wine into your glasses, cider in an old tin can,
Put John Barleycorn in a nut-brown bowl,
For he proved the strongest man.

What came first, the hymn or the drinking song, I don't know, but the time of the harvest was a good time to be in the choir.

I also attended Sunday School at the church. The teacher was a Swinford local, and she told us young folks that the cross of holy water that the vicar marked on our foreheads at baptism could never be washed, or even scrubbed, off. It was there forever, burned into our skin. I firmly believed this at the time—but in those days I pretty much believed whatever any grown-up told me.

Italian prisoners of war, some of whom helped with the farm work, wandered quite freely around the village, even hanging out at the pubs. They wore brown jumpsuits with large colored patches sewn on them. The patches were intended to be shooting targets in case the prisoners should try to run off, but none of them ever did. Why would they? They were safely away from the war, and who would shoot them anyway? Apart from the occasional farmer with a rusty old shotgun that he would use for bagging rabbits, no one was armed, and, in general, the villagers were quite friendly with the Italians. The German prisoners of war were locked up somewhere, though; we never saw any of those men. I have been told that a couple of the Italian prisoners, and one German, stayed and settled in the village after the war.

Apart from the Italian prisoners and the news on the radio, there was little in Swinford to indicate that there was a war on, although I do remember that a Lancaster bomber crashed near to the village, and, after school, we all ran to see the wreckage. There was a bloody flying jacket that some of the boys tried on, but not me.

There were also gun emplacement areas in the fields around the village, but no guns. Children often used the earth embankments around the emplacement areas to play Hide and Seek. A major railway hub in the market town of Rugby, just six miles away, amazingly escaped an attack from German bombs, which would have been devastating to the British war effort. Meanwhile, in the tiny village of Stanford, just two miles from Swinford, a stately home called Stanford Hall became a safe house for nuns from a convent in London, and for the population of a London girls' school. We saw some British soldiers and airmen from time to time, and once in a while an American soldier or airman. The American was a rarity, and if one was spotted, he would be pursued by children calling out, "Got any gum, chum?" A stick of American chewing gum was a real prize, and those GIs invariably came through.

Food rationing was in force all over Britain, but folks who lived in the countryside were better off than those who lived in the towns. They were able to grow some staples such as potatoes and carrots, and keep livestock. I do not remember food shortages in Swinford. Of course, even in war-torn London, some folks had allotments. How the English people love their allotments! Posters were placed all over Britain with the slogan *Dig for Victory*. Some showed a spade being driven into the ground, others, happy healthy people tending their Victory gardens. For children, sweets and candy were rationed, which, given the quality of dental care at the time, was probably a good thing. We had ration books that contained cut-out coupons that we traded, or used in the village confectioner's. Offords Sweet Shop, it was called. I went to the village school with a boy named Maurice, who was an Offord. He was a very quiet boy, and the teachers were a bit hard on him. When he had to do a writing exercise, he wrote nothing more on his paper than *Maurice*.

My aunts, Nellie and Edie, and Uncle Arthur, came to Swinford for a visit. It was a few days away from the Blitz for them, and quite exciting. I think they all stayed in the Hornsby house. Aunt Edie was a young and very attractive widow; her sailor husband, uncle Alf, had died of an illness. He was very handsome and played the harmonica in a Royal Navy band. She brought her daughter, my five-year-old cousin Patricia, with her. Patricia had a great time chasing the piglets. Aunt Nellie's husband was a prisoner of war in Poland, and Arthur was drafted into the army shortly after his visit.

While in Swinford, we got news that our rented house in Rural Place, New Cross, had been destroyed by a bomb. Only my father was in London and in Rural Place, but fortunately, he was in an air raid shelter when the bombers came. My mother, who was in Swinford at the time, told us the news. A neighbor in Rural Place, Harry Weller, was also bombed out. He quickly found another house to rent a few streets away, at 28 Lausanne Road. He asked Mum and Dad if they would like to move in with him and his girlfriend, Nora. Mum and Dad said yes, and they did, dividing up the house for two families—an arrangement that would last for forty years.

In early 1941, my brother was accepted into a very good school, Lutterworth Grammar, so for awhile he commuted from Swinford to Lutterworth. Sometime later he transferred to a famous school with a grand name—Aske's Hatcham Haberdashers Grammar School for Boys, a South East London school near to Lausanne Road. The students and faculty of Aske's were moved, *en masse* and for the duration of the war, to Teignmouth, in glorious Devon. My brother was billeted there with a family of poachers (at least that's what he told *us!*).

A Short Return to London

I did move back to London to be with my parents for a while, and I'm not sure when I did, or why. There may have been a lull in the bombing. We were already living in the Lausanne Road house, and I went to the elementary school in Waller Road. Like many Londoners, we had an Anderson shelter in the back garden. If you did not have much money, the government would give you a shelter; otherwise, you would pay a few pounds for it. The shelter was made of straight and curved corrugated steel plates, which, when bolted together, formed an inverted U. This assembly was placed in a four-foot-deep pit in the back or front garden, and was then covered with soil on top. Sandbags were placed around the sides and an opening was left for the doorway. About three feet of soil was recommended for the top of the shelter, just right for growing tomato plants. Londoners, like all English people, like growing plants and flowers, and the top of the shelter was the perfect place.

I have heard that there were organized competitions for shelters with the best floral arrangements, but I think you needed something more exotic than tomato plants to compete. We were not in that league. The dimensions of the shelter were 6'6" long, 4'6" wide, and 6'0" high. It was quite snug, and smelly at times. They were built to fit six people, and that would be a very tight fit. There were seven folks in our house, but two were children, my cousin Patricia and me: then there were my parents; Mum's younger sister, Aunt Edie; Harry, the guy upstairs and his girlfriend Nora. My brother was with his school in Devon.

Patricia's dad, Uncle Alf, had been in the Royal Navy, and we had two of his sailor hats, which we lined with newspaper. Patricia and I wore them and felt quite safe. Apart from bunk beds, there were some essential needs when in the shelter—an oil lamp, some contraption for heating water to make tea (which no Londoner could last for long without), and a chamber pot.

Folks who did not have an Anderson shelter could go to a public facility. These were usually brick structures called Morrison Shelters. Another option were the deep-underground tube stations. Thousands of people slept on the platforms, but this option was not as safe as many believed, and there were many fatalities. Of course, there were those who, when they heard the whine of the air raid warning siren, just stayed in their houses, but we headed for our Anderson Shelter. During night-time raids, this had to be done in the dark—it was an offense to show even the tiniest chink of light, and doing so would bring down the wrath of the Air Raid Warning Police (ARP). They would walk around the streets at night, blowing whistles and banging on doors to tell people to keep their curtains drawn. At the start of the Blitz, the blackout was so strictly enforced that more people were injured by walking into lamp posts, than by bombs. The authorities had to make some adjustments. As far as the German pilots were concerned, all they needed was the moon and a cloudless sky. The German pilots would follow the moonlit Thames to the docklands and the City of London, and there, they would drop their bombs. Bad weather was London's best defense.

Many of the men, most of them too old to be in the military, never actually went into the shelters. They stood outside during a raid to watch the action in the sky. Some of them, like my dad, who had very bad eyesight, were in the Home Guard and stood on rooftops to watch for fires. They had tin hats and maybe an ancient rifle just in case. Dad had told me that, even with his poor eyesight, he was quite a good shot with what was called a Bren gun. As for the other men, there was not much point in them leaving their houses. They puffed on their pipes and cigarettes and pontificated on all aspects of the war. When a plane flew overhead, they had the uncanny ability to tell if it was friend or foe. "One of ours," one would assure us. The others would mumble their agreement. How could they possibly tell? I don't know, but their confidence was probably reassuring to those in earshot.

The All Clear, a long single note of the siren, sent everyone scrambling back into their houses, where, before anything else, the kettle went on the stove for that vital cup of tea.

There was a ritual for making tea. Heat the teapot by holding it over the steaming kettle spout, then put one spoonful of tea in it for each drinker and then one for the pot. Wartime rationing called for omitting the "one for the pot." The boiling water was poured directly onto the loose tea leaves, and it was then left to "brew" for four or five, minutes. The longer it brewed the stronger it became. Very strong tea was referred to as "Builder's Tea." A snack usually went with the tea, maybe some bread and fake butter. The bread was usually gray in color and came from what was called the "national loaf"; unless you bought from local bakers, that was the only kind of bread you could get in wartime Britain, but it was healthy. It was basically whole wheat bread, as opposed to the pre-war white bread that was nutritionally useless.

People, however, were not fond of the national loaf. They longed for the war to be over, and for the return of white bread. In spite of food rationing—or maybe because of it—it has been said that Londoners were better nourished during the war than before or after. One factor was the national loaf.

One alternative to tea was coffee, though not many British people drank it in those days; for those who did, there was something called "camp coffee," a dark-brown mixture that came in a square bottle. You poured a little of it into a cup, then poured hot water on it, and *voila!* you had coffee. An amusing story circulated that featured English coffee and the great French general Charles De Gaulle. The General had escaped to England when France fell to the German Army in 1940. On his arrival, he was offered a hot drink. He took a sip and said, "So this is your English tea." The answer was, "No General, this is our English coffee."

For young children who did not have full comprehension of what was going on, there was some excitement in those air raids. Searchlights, flares, loud explosions, and barrage balloons: It was tempting for a young person to try to sneak out of the shelters to join the men watching the action in the sky, but mothers would pull them back from the shelter steps. I remember seeing a German bomber caught in the glare of three or four searchlights, with shells exploding around it. The plane was desperately twisting and turning to escape back into the darkness and out of sight of the anti-aircraft gunners. I don't know what the success rate was for the gunners, but it could not have been very high. But if the guns were not very accurate, they were very loud.

The morning after an air raid, children searched in the streets and gardens for shrapnel—the jagged fragments of bomb or shell casings. A complete nose cone of one or the other was a prize find, something for a show-and-tell at school, maybe even to make a trade. Some of the teachers were very severe and seemed to like caning small children, so it was best to wait for mid-morning break before showing off one's collection. The problem was, we could not tell if a piece of shrapnel came from a bomb or a shell. If we could have done that, we would have known which pieces came from "one of ours."

Return to Swinford

After some months, I was returned to Swinford, where I was to spend the rest of the war. I don't know how it happened.

Back in the village, I was billeted with the Page family. Mr. Page was a Batman in the Royal Air Force—a personal servant to an officer. He rode off on his bike every morning to wherever his job was. Mrs. Page kept house and suffered from terrible asthma. It often seemed that she could not breathe at all, and her loud gasps to take in air were quite frightening. Sometimes, she had to have medical attention. I remember, one very cold winter night when there was heavy snow on the ground, Mrs. Page had a serious attack, and Mr. Page had to go to the one public telephone in the village and call a doctor. The doctor came in a horse-drawn sleigh. He had traveled for some miles in the dark and snow to perform his medical duties.

The Pages had three children, the eldest a girl, followed by two boys, the older of whom was about my age, nine years old at this point. The government gave some money to families that took in children, about ten shillings a week, I think it was, and sometimes parents added a little more. I went back to the village school and entered Miss Mechim's class. I had by then learned to read and write, and that's when I became a choir boy. However, we still made hooked rugs.

The Page home was one of five terraced cottages. They were all probably "tied" cottages—owned, that is, by a farmer or landowner who employed the people who lived in them, so those people paid rent to their employer. If they left their employment, they lost their home. The cottage was very small; it had one room and a scullery downstairs, and two rooms upstairs. There was no electricity or indoor plumbing. Water was supplied by a communal pump at the back of the cottages and by rain barrels placed under the roof gutters. The rainwater was said to be "soft water"; I don't quite know what that meant, but it was the water of choice for washing clothes. There were three outhouses for five families, about thirty yards behind the cottages. Once every two or three weeks, a horse-drawn cart came by, and the driver hauled away the filled outhouse bins and replaced them with empty bins. What a job. In the winter, the walk to the outhouse was not pleasant: One had to be warmly dressed before leaving the house. The toilet paper was torn up pieces of old newspaper, mostly from the *Daily Mirror*, and there was no lighting.

All hot meals were cooked over a wood fire, which also heated the house. There was no other source of heat, and in the winter, the upstairs rooms were bitterly cold. After school, I went with the Page children to borrow a pram from a family across the street. We took it to the fields to gather firewood. This took some time, but we always managed to fill the pram. Sometime we were lucky enough to find some pieces of coal on the road that had fallen off a lorry. We were not bothered by stuff like homework, so when our chores were over, we were free to do whatever we wanted. I went to join my two best friends in the village, Roland Barnet and Dave Hotchkiss.

Roland, Dave, and I were a pretty tight trio and spent most evenings and weekends together. A popular pastime for children was "scrumping," that is, taking fruit from trees that belonged to someone else. Most farmers did not mind if you picked up the "fallens," fruit lying on the ground, but they did not like you picking from their trees. But hanging fruit is the best, so I confess we did pick from the trees, but only those at the orchard's edge. With a 'leg up', one of us was able to reach some apples, plums, or pears.

Dave was very inventive and good at making things. He once made crossbows for the three of us. They were quite lethal weapons, especially when loaded with arrows made from sharpened umbrella spokes. Paper flights were glued on to the arrows so that they would fly straight. I am not sure how it happened, but Roland once had a loaded bow, and his finger must have slipped off the trigger. The arrow flew loose and struck me in the back of my head. It stuck there. I can't remember my reaction, but it must have been something close to panic; after all, it is not every day you have an arrow stuck in your head. Luckily, I was facing away from Roland, or it could have been very bad indeed. Dave pulled out the arrow and took away our crossbows.

Sixty years later, when visiting Swinford, I met up with Roland. He asked me how I was; I said I was in good shape. He asked me about the arrow. He wanted to know if I had had any bad effects from having it stuck in my head. "Don't think so," I said. Roland was relieved. He said he had been waking up at night for sixty years, worried that he might have damaged my life by shooting me in the head. I assured him that I was OK, and had no ill effects; on reflection, I thought it *might* explain a thing or two. But I didn't tell Roland that.

It was well known that delicious wild strawberries flourished on the railway embankments near Swinford. It was a long walk, along a narrow path through dark woods and an abandoned quarry, to get to the railway tracks, but woods are always mysterious, and I think we imagined we were on some great adventure of exploration. We did hope to see an express train on its way from London to Scotland, maybe even see the Flying Scotsman, which to us, was the most famous train in the world.

On the embankments, we picked from the harvest of wild strawberries, and ate many of them. We tried to take some home by putting them in our pockets, but that did not work out too well. Apart from the disaster of crushed strawberries and stained clothing, we were roundly scolded for being out so late, and so close to the railway tracks. We were forbidden to go back to those embankments . . .but I think we did.

Bath night was interesting. The government let the British people know that, when taking a bath, the maximum depth of water should not exceed five inches. To reinforce the policy, they pointed out that King George used only five inches of water. The King's patriotism was impressive, but then he had a bathtub, and he probably took a bath every day. We, like most families, had a small tin bath that hung behind the scullery door. It was taken down every two weeks, put on the floor in front of the fireplace, and half filled with hot water that had been heated over the wood fire. A clothes horse with towels draped over it was placed around the bath to provide a modicum of privacy to the bathers. Then the three boys and one girl would take turns in bathing in the tub, all in the same water— a bit rough for the last one in. I don't know what the grown ups did for a bath; I have no recollection of them ever taking one. To this day, I have no idea of *why* water was subject to rationing—it is something Britain has more than enough of. Maybe they were trying to conserve the fuel used to heat the water. (But in our case that would merely have been the fallen wood that we had gathered.)

There were times when Mr. and Mrs. Page had very noisy rows, usually when they came home from the pub. He was quite dramatic. He would call his children down from the bedroom, line them up, and tell them that he had been a good father to them, but as he and their mother could no longer get along, he would have to leave. He said that, once he stepped outside the front door, he would never come back. "Good!" said Mrs. P.

"I mean it," said he.

"You know where the door is," she said.

It always ended the same way: He would leave the house and go out into the night, then, twenty minutes later, he would be back. They'd have a cup of tea, and that was that.

All four of us children shared one bedroom and one chamber pot, while Mr. and Mrs. Page had the other bedroom and their own chamber pot. Carrying those pots down the stairs in the morning was a risky business. While we were getting up in the mornings and getting ready to go to school, Mrs. Page would call out to us the latest news from the front. She would get the news from the radio (or the wireless, as it was called). It was always good news, so it seemed we were winning all of the time. The wireless was vital—the link to news and entertainment, it's what kept the country together.

Recreation

The wireless offered two programs: the BBC Home Service, and the BBC Light Program. We listened to the singing of Vera Lynn, and to Tommy Handley telling jokes and stories on his famous show called *ITMA* (*It's That Man Again*). Bing Crosby, The Inkspots, and the Andrew Sisters were enormously popular. At 4:00 p.m., the children's hour came on, with Winnie the Pooh and my favorite, the adventures of Larry the Lamb and his friend Denis the Dachshund. Larry and Dennis lived in Toytown along with Ernest the Policeman, Mr. Growser the Grocer, the Inventor, and many others.

There was a cinema somewhere too, but I can't remember where. It could have been in Lutterworth or Rugby. The programs at the cinema were long and consisted of a main feature film, a secondary feature film, usually an American Western, some cartoons, and then a newsreel. The latter kept us up to date on what was going on in the war, or rather what the government wanted the people to know about it. As I recall, we usually saw the British forces winning the war all by themselves. Scenes of Italian soldiers with their hands up, running to surrender, brought gales of laughter from the audience. To be fair to the Italian soldiers, it was edited propaganda film designed to boost the morale of the British population. The American and Russian forces got some mentions, but not as much as General Montgomery. The national anthem was always played at the end of a film show. Some folks tried to get out of the cinema before the anthem started so they would not have to stand still for two or three minutes.

Reading was a great escape. I enjoyed the stories by the children's author Enid Blyton. I recall her book *Five on a Treasure Island* as a gripping read. The Biggles books by W. E. Johns were great favorites. Biggles was a fighter pilot, and he, along with his pals, Algy and Ginger, thwarted the Nazis and enemy agents at every turn. I think I read all of the *Just William* stories, by Richmal

Crompton. The school boy William and his friends were constantly in and out of trouble, and it was easy to see oneself in William's shoes. A weekly comic book, called *The Champion*, was very popular, and one featured character was Rockfist Rogan. Rockfist was, like Biggles, a fighter pilot, but where ever he found himself in the war, he always had a pair of boxing gloves with him. On his adventures, he often met up with a German counterpart who also went around with his boxing gloves. The two of them would take a time out from the war to have a boxing match. When they had finished, they put their gloves away and went back to the war. Shouldn't Rockfist have tried to *capture* the German guy? I thought so. A number of the heroic figures in these stories, like Biggles and Rockfist, were portrayed as coming from very aristocratic backgrounds. I didn't think much about it at the time, but Britain was a very class-ridden society during the 1940s and remained so for a long time after. I remember my grandmother, Ada Jones, née Skeels, telling me that the "upper classes" were "born to rule."

The End Is in Sight

I took, and failed, my eleven-plus exam in late 1944, so there was no grammar school for me. If the exam had been about hooked rugs, I would have passed with flying colors. Unfortunately, one had to know something about arithmetic and some other subjects. All I can remember is that I could not understand any of the questions on the exam paper.

The war was still going on, but the morning news from Mrs. Page was getting better. The Prime Minister, Winston Churchill, President Roosevelt, and Uncle Joe Stalin, seemed to have a good handle on things. These three, known as "The Big Three," were considered heroes. There is no doubt that they were mighty men, but they had flaws. Years later we learned that Stalin, who had been portrayed as this jolly old fellow whom everyone would want at their children's Christmas party, was, in fact, one of the greatest mass murderers in human history. Everybody liked the American President, and when parents and guardians wanted to get children to go to bed, they would say to them, "If you don't go to bed, you will get rings under your eyes like Mr. Roosevelt."

On the morning of Tuesday, May 8, 1945, Mrs. Page shouted up the stairs that the war in Europe was over, and that we had won. It was a school day, and we did not get the day off—we went to school as usual and probably made hooked rugs. What a great morning.

Swinford only had one streetlight. You can be sure, however, that that evening, the light was turned on, and the people of Swinford gathered under it to celebrate.

Very soon after, we evacuees said goodbye to our friends and those who had looked after us, and we went home. I can't remember anything about the journey back to London, but I returned to 28 Lausanne Road and to school in Waller Road for a few months. My brother returned with his school, from Devon, and the school moved back to its old quarters at the top of Pepys Road in New Cross. My mother's brothers, Ernie and Arthur, would soon be back from Europe, released from their service in the army. Her brother Charlie had been transferred from the army to the coal mines in Wales; he was a "Bevin Boy," so called for the British wartime Minister of Labour Ernest Bevin. He would go back to his old job as a bricklayer. My dad's younger brother, Bill, was released from his army service as well, and Dad would be free from his home guard duties.

Aunt Nellie's husband, Uncle Dave Austin, had been called up soon after their wedding in 1939, and had been captured at Dunkirk. He had spent five years as a prisoner of war at Stalag XXID in Poland. The Germans had grabbed him in 1940 while he was fighting in a rearguard action near to the Dunkirk beaches. He fought with his regiment, the Queens Own Royal West Kent, 7th Battalion. His unit was all but wiped out; but Uncle Dave was lucky to have been one of the few survivors. I have a video recording of him describing this action in vivid detail, including the surviving soldiers having to watch as the Germans shot their commanding officer, Captain Hill, before their eyes. At one point, Dave and his mates were lined up against a wall and expected to be shot themselves, but a German officer came along and gave them a reprieve. Uncle Dave had kept a diary from childhood, and he posted a record of the events for every day of active duty he was involved in, and for every day he spent in captivity. His unit was given credit for holding off the German forces long enough to enable more Allied soldiers to get back to England. In 1945, in the chaos created by the invasion, he and some of his fellow prisoners had simply walked away from their internment and made their way across Europe, hoping to meet up with the American army. On the way, some Slovakian partisans had given Uncle Dave and his mates a lorry to speed them across Europe. Soon he would be home.

One of our family members would not come home. On August 19, 1942, William "Bibbo" Stubbs, from Dad's family, had been killed while on a bombing mission. The story given by the authorities was that his plane had crashed into the North Sea in mysterious circumstances, and the crew were killed. That may be true, but on that same day, August 19th, there was a combined raid by British,

Canadian, and American forces, on the German occupied port of Dieppe, in Northern France. As far as the Allies were concerned, it was a disaster. The Germans had early warning, and were ready for the raid. The Royal Airforce lost 106 aircraft in that raid, and 6000 allied troops, mostly Canadians, were killed or captured. Was Bibbo's plane flying to Dieppe to be a part of that raid? We shall never know.

Bibbo and his comrades are remembered with honor on a fine memorial that was erected for airmen of the Commonwealth. It is located in Runnymead, Surrey, near to where King John, surrounded by his Barons, signed the Magna Carta in 1215.

So there we were—Aunt Edie with her daughter Patricia, now about seven years old; Harry was still upstairs, but his girlfriend, Aunt Nora, had tired of him and moved out. Harry was very quiet. He crept around the house so softly, no one could hear him coming. Aunt Edie called him "Creeping Jesus." He proposed marriage to Edie, but she turned "Creeping Jesus" down.

There had been heavy damage to properties in the neighborhood around 28 Lausanne. Rural Place was no more—it had completely disappeared from the map. The houses had been so badly damaged that they all had to be totally removed. The shops around the corner from Rural Place survived the bombing and were still in business but were torn down after the war to make way for development. Some very bad decisions were made when it came to demolishing bomb-damaged buildings. Many fine houses that could have been saved and restored were knocked down and replaced with drab and inferior construction. Number 28 had survived with no more than light damage, although adjacent houses had been completely demolished. When the debris from the bomb sites had been removed, many were used for allotments until new houses could be built. A friendly neighbor who used his share of an allotment to grow vegetables would come over to our house for a cup of tea. He always brought something he had grown, usually string beans.

My mother's sisters, Lily, Edie, and Nelly, often came to Number 28 to help tame the wild growth in our very long back garden. They cut the grass with garden shears, raked the flower beds, picked fruit from the apple and pear trees, sipped tea, and talked. The war in Europe was over, and there was great relief.

My dear aunt Lily, the oldest of my mother's siblings, was happy that her younger brothers, Charlie, Ernie, and Arthur, and her brother-in-law Dave, would soon be home, especially her youngest brother, Arthur. She had cared for him since their parents, who, as I have previously mentioned, did not live past their forties, died. Arthur was just a babe in arms at the time. Aunt Lily had heard something on the radio about the weight of the backpacks and equipment that a soldier had to carry, and she thought of her brothers. She said that Winston Churchill "needed a job" and a "good talking to" for making her brothers carry such heavy loads all across Europe. She was right, of course. Aunt Lily, the rock of our family, was always right. Lily and Arthur never married; they spent the rest of their lives looking after each other. Lily died first, but my mother, and her brothers and sisters, were not far away, so Arthur was never alone.

Final Thoughts

With my wife, Louise, I have made a number of visits to Swinford in recent years and have met with Roland, Mary, and Jean. They are all contented with their village lives, and they have helped

Coming back to Swinford in 2005. Left to right: Mary Barnett's husband Bernard; Mary Barnett; Mary, wife of Roland Barnett; Roland Barnett; me; and Jean Hornsby

me in reviving memories of life in a village that, over the years, has barely changed at all, although the population has exploded to five hundred, and the village now has only one pub.

I have read that some studies show that children who were not evacuated from the cities, but stayed in their own homes with their parents, often grew up to be better-adjusted individuals than those who were sent away to live with strangers. I don't know what the truth of that is, but I do know that today's parents would not permit their children to be taken away from them without knowing a lot more about what was going on. Today, we know that the folks in government don't always know what is best.

I have met former evacuees who claim that being evacuated was a life-changing experience for the better. They left wretched and unhappy homes in the cities and found a new way of life in the country. Many of them stayed in touch with their foster families and have good and happy memories. For others, the opposite is true, and their memories are painful. The time of greatest stress seems to have been on the very first day of the evacuation, when children were taken away from their homes, transported to places they knew nothing about, gathered in village halls and other assembly points, where they sat, waiting to be "selected" by would-be foster parents. A memory that is still difficult, eighty years later.

THE BLACKBERRY-AND-APPLE PIE

A Reminiscence of Potato Picking In Wartime England

BLACKBERRIES AND APPLES RIPEN at about the same time of the year, in late September; soon after, potato-picking season rolls around. I imagine it is the same wherever blackberries, apples, and potatoes grow, and that's the way it was, and still is, in the midlands of England. Wild fruits flourish, especially blackberries, which grow in the hedgerows, and most farmers don't mind if you pick up the fallen apples—they are still very good. As for potatoes, not many folks go out for a pleasant day of picking them up, but it was a way to add to the meager incomes of most country folk, and the companionship was usually good.

During World War II, many agriculture workers had been called up for military service. Others had left farming for better-paying jobs in munition factories and other companies related to the war effort, so there was a serious labor shortage on the farms, and attempts were launched to make up for them. Some of these included the Woman's Land Army, which was made up of young women with some training in farm work. Italian prisoners of war worked on the farms, and they earned money for their work—about three shillings a day, I think it was. I have heard of German prisoners who did some farm work, but I can't recall seeing any. Farm camps were advertised with posters of happy, smiling workers and slogans with variants of *Lend a hand with the potato harvest.* These camps offered a chance for a working holiday and for townsfolk to enjoy the countryside for a week or two. If they were from London, it offered the prospect of respite from the bombing.

There were also School Harvest Camps, so that school children could work on the land. Fruit and potato picking is not highly skilled work, and young folks can be very effective pickers.

In Swinford, as I recall, it was mostly local folk, villagers and school children, with some Italian prisoners and a few women from the Land Army, who helped with the potato crop.

When the picking season came in the autumn, a number of Swinford school children joined the pickers at local farms to add a few shillings to whatever pocket money they got. I went potato picking for the Simon family, an important family in the village of Swinford and in the farming community. They had the largest farm in the locality and were pillars of the local church.

I was nine years old at the time, and I got up very early in the morning and dressed warmly, as it was early October and Old Man Winter was taking his first bites. I waited outside the house where I was living for the lorry that would take me and other children to the fields. I had been offered some sandwiches by the lady of the house—she did tell me that it would be a very long day and I would get hungry—but I declined her offer. I suppose I didn't see the point of sandwiches as I wasn't hungry at the time, but I also did not like the idea of carrying sandwiches in a paper bag. I don't know why; maybe I thought it would make me look silly. Looking back, not taking the sandwiches was the silly part, but it seems I had not yet learned to take good advice and listen to grownups who knew a lot more than I did. Simply put, I had not learned to look ahead.

The lorry came and stopped right where I stood. I pulled myself up into the open back, which was already almost filled with children, many sitting on the floor while others stood, hanging on to whatever they could, and off we went to the potato fields. It was a bumpy ride, and there were no seat belts.

When we arrived at the fields, we tumbled out and assembled with the other pickers, mostly local village people and children. in the large farm house kitchen. We were each given a bucket to put the potatoes in and told where to empty it when it was full. Then we were taken out to the field to be assigned a row and set to work.

The ground had been turned over and the potatoes thrown to the surface by a magical machine called a *spinner*, which was basically an assemblage of whirling blades that whipped the potatoes from the ground. So they were mostly exposed and lying on the surface of the soil, where they were easy to pick up.

When the bucket was full, I carried it back to the end of the row and emptied it into a large container. It was hard work because you had to be bent over from the waist for much of the working day. How many potatoes in a day a young boy or girl could pick up, I don't know, but some of the younger folks were very fast and enthusiastic, so I suppose, with enough of us working, at the end of the day it was worth it to the farmer.

After a long morning at work, lunchtime came, and again we

gathered in the farm house kitchen. There was a large wooden table in the center of the room laden with plates, pots, and loaves of crusty bread. The young Mr. Simon, a burly and cheerful man, sat at this table; his mother, a plump, rosy- cheeked woman who was a prominent figure in the village church, was scurrying around, making sure that her son had enough to eat. The adult workers found various places to eat their sandwiches and drink their tea, while the young folks sat on the floor around the perimeter of the kitchen. They leaned their backs against the wall to eat their sandwiches and drink whatever beverage they had brought with them. . .all except one. I didn't have any sandwiches or anything to drink, and by then I was very hungry.

After Mr. Simon had had his main course, his mother brought him his dessert, or, as we would say in those days, his "afters," a large bowl of steaming hot blackberry-and-apple pie topped with thick yellow custard, the most delicious, mouth- watering pie a young boy, or anyone come to that, could possibly have imagined. It was magnificent. My memories of how wonderful English custard was may have been enhanced over the years, but it was very good. She put the bowl down on the table in front of him; he picked up his spoon and began to consume large, delicious mouthfuls. My eyes were fixed on him, and I *so* wanted a piece of that pie.

At that moment, he looked around at the boys and girls eating their sandwiches and saw that I had nothing. "What's up, lad?" he asked in a broad Midlands accent. "Hast thee no sandwiches?"

"N-no," I stammered. "I never get hungry in the middle of the day," a fatal mistake to have made—I had put myself in a hole that I probably could not get out of.

"Well, thee must have something to eat lad," he insisted. "There's still an afternoon's work to do." He turned to his mother and said, "Mother, give young lad a piece of pie."

What was I to do? I had said I never get hungry in the middle of the day, but I did want a piece of that pie. I struggled to say, "Yes, thank you," but what came out was, "No, it's all right. I don't like to eat in the middle of the day."

Neither he nor his mother believed this absurd statement and tried to persuade me to change my mind, but somehow, I couldn't. I don't know why, but I was unable to say, "Oh, yes, I would *love* a piece of pie." So they gave up, and soon we went back to picking potatoes.

At the end of the day I stood in line with the other children to collect the one shilling and sixpence that was due to each of us. It was a fixed amount, no matter how many buckets you filled. The adult pickers got more, but then, they probably picked up more potatoes. I had not eaten since breakfast at 7:00 a.m., and it was then about 4:00 p.m. My stomach was groaning, and I was starving. With a shilling and a sixpenny piece in my pocket, I climbed back onto the lorry and found a place to sit on the wooden floor with the other children. The bumpy ride back to Swinford made my empty stomach feel even worse. The long working day was over.

That potato field, the farmhouse kitchen, and the memory of that hot blackberry-and-apple pie with the thick creamy yellow custard, haunts me to this day, some seventy plus years later. Why couldn't I have said, "Yes, thank you, I would love a piece of pie!" I don't know, but at least I have very fond memories of Mr. Simon and his very nice mother.

BIBBICOT KIM AND HER MORNING TEA

NGLISH PEOPLE DO LIKE THEIR CUPS OF TEA, especially first thing in the morning. As this story demonstrates—sometimes, so do English dogs, or perhaps dogs that belong to English people, as dogs probably do not have a nationality.

Soon after the end of World War II in Europe, when I was about ten years old, my uncles, Albert Skeels and Bill Stubbs, with their wives Mary and Jenny, decided to leave the East End of London and emigrate to South Africa.

Albert had a reputation for knowing how to make money. He was a great talker and a bit of an operator—he bought green grocery stores that were not doing well, built up the businesses, and then sold them at a profit. Bill Stubbs was a window cleaner. Many in our family believed that Albert was rich. I don't think he was, but he was probably better off than the rest. He wasn't free with his money, but he wasn't a miser either. I do remember that he once gave me two shillings and sixpence for Christmas, which at the time was a useful sum of money.

I don't remember Albert and Mary having any children, but Bill

*Uncles and aunts with Bibbo. Left to right, Uncles Bob and Bill Stubbs,
Aunts Jenny and Ada. Bibbo is in the front.*

and Jenny had a son named William (known in family circles as
"Bibbo"), an only child who, as already been told, was killed in
World War II.

I don't know how or why they reached the decision to emigrate;
they were not young people looking for adventure. They were all
well into middle age and quite settled in their ways. Maybe as far
as Bill and Jenny were concerned, it was a way to start over and as-
suage their grief over the loss of their son, or perhaps they all just
wanted to get away from the drab austerity of post-war Britain.
Whatever the reason, they were leaving.

But Bill and Jenny had a problem to solve before they could
leave England. They owned a beautiful, pure-bred black spaniel

named Kim; her kennel name was Bibbicot Kim. They were very attached to her and had to find a good home for her before they could leave the country. Uncle Bill asked my parents if they would adopt her and look after her. They said they would be happy to. So one day, Uncle Bill brought Kim to our house in Lausanne Road. She was not a young dog, but she was beautiful and very friendly. We all looked forward to having her in our house.

Before Dad and Uncle Bill got around to discussing Kim's likes, dislikes, and needs, Dad made some sandwiches and the all-important pot of tea. He probably made the very strong tea, known as "builder's tea," tea so strong that a spoon would stand up in it. After all, Dad was a plasterer, and Uncle Bill was a window cleaner. Not much got accomplished in England, or even started, in those days before a cuppa. The first words a visitor would hear from a host were "I'll put the kettle on." With their sandwiches and tea, Dad and Bill sat down in our small back room to discuss Kim's future. We actually had quite a large house—three floors and eight rooms, plus an enormous back garden, but my parents, like so many other working-class Londoners, always preferred the back room. For many folks, including some of my aunts, the front room was reserved for guests and contained the best furniture, which was usually covered with sheets so that no one would sit on the chairs—that is, if they were allowed in the front room at all. It was like a holy inner sanctum. In the case of Dad and Bill, it may have been the back room was used because it was closer to the kitchen, or that the large rear window gave a fine view of the garden.

After awhile, Uncle Bill got around to explaining what Kim liked, what she didn't like, and what she absolutely had to have. She was quite easygoing and happy with most things, but what she positively had to have, was an early morning cup of tea. Uncle Bill very earnestly explained to Dad, "She do like 'er cuppa first thing in the mornin'." Bill, like everyone in our family, was a Cockney. He repeated many times the importance of a morning cup of tea for Kim, and Dad assured him that she would always get one, served in a saucer of course, when he made the morning tea—and he was true to his word. Kim would lap up that saucer of morning tea with relish, wagging her tail while she did. I don't think Kim got builder's tea, that might have been a bit too strong for her. Fortunately, though, Kim was not really interested in how the tea was made, just in the lapping.

When all of her needs had been discussed, the sandwiches eaten, and the tea drunk, Uncle Bill got up to say goodbye. He gave Kim a farewell hug, put his coat on, then walked with Mum and Dad out through the front door to the garden gate. They chatted for awhile. I don't know what they talked about; maybe they reminisced about family and the old days on the Isle of Dogs. I have often wondered whether it occurred to the three of them at that time that it was to be goodbye forever. After some final words and a peck on the check for Mum, Bill turned, opened the gate, and strolled down Lausanne Road to the bus stop on Queens Road. Kim, and our family, would never see him again, and Kim was now our dog.

Uncles Albert and Bill, with Aunts Mary and Jenny, went off to South Africa, and Kim stayed with us. She *was* an easygoing dog and settled in very quickly as one of the family, but like all retriever dogs, she had a passion for chasing and retrieving objects that were thrown for her. I took to throwing stones as far as I could in our long back garden, and she ran and searched with great enthusiasm to find the stone, and then brought it back, pushing it forward with her nose for another throw. She never tired of this, but I, and other people who threw stones for her, did. Our only escape was to retreat into the house. Kim lived a contented life with us for the years she had left, until she died.

The uncles and aunts eventually left South Africa and moved on to Australia. Why they left, I don't know, but early in the 1950s, the draconian system of apartheid was being strictly enforced in South Africa, and the situation was becoming ugly. They got themselves out of there, hopefully because they did not want to live under that wretched system, but maybe because Albert simply saw better opportunities in Australia. They moved to Melbourne, where they all lived a good life until, eventually, time took its toll. Mary, Albert, and Bill died, I don't know in what order, and Aunt Jenny found herself alone. With her cat and dog, she lived a solitary life in her Melbourne house until she was well into her nineties, and then, it seems, she felt a yearning to go home. She wanted to return to England to be near her family and her East London roots—a brave decision at her age. She had a much younger cousin named Dolly, who flew out from England to Melbourne to help settle her affairs in Australia and to bring her on the long journey back to London. Jenny lived with Dolly until it became clear to all that she needed more care than Dolly could possibly provide, so it was arranged for her to move to a very fine nursing home near to Aylesbury, in Buckinghamshire.

I took my dad to the home to visit Aunt Jenny several times. My aunt Ada, Dad's younger sister, was also a very faithful visitor. The nurses, true to the English way, always brought us pots of tea and biscuits, and Jenny shared memories of her life in Australia, a country she had clearly come to love. She also liked to talk about the old days in the East End of London, and of the fruit and vegetable trade that she and her family had been involved in. She was a classic Cockney, and the nurses, who called her Jane, her real name, loved her spirit. She would tell them, "Don't worry about me, look after the others." On her bedside table stood a photograph of Bibbo. It was nestled alongside a vase of fresh flowers. Eventually, at more than a hundred years old, she died in that home.

Now, these many years later, I wonder about these aunts and uncles. Were they happier in their new countries than they would have been had they stayed in England? While the four of them were together, I suppose they were all right—they had company—but the last few years, after Albert, Bill, and Mary died, must have been very hard for Jenny. I am sure that she had friends, but there was no extended family to help her out, no one to talk to about the old days. When Jenny was alone, she sent Dad the fare for him to fly out to Australia to visit her. He went, but the long and tedious flight was really too much for him. He did not like to recline his seat back, feeling that it would inconvenience the passenger behind him, so he sat upright for the twenty-plus hours of the flight. He was well into his mid-eighties, and when he returned to London he was totally exhausted and never fully recovered from the stress of that trip. He said that mostly he had spent four weeks sitting in Jenny's back room, drinking cups of tea and eating sandwiches, just as he would have done in the back room of his own house in Lausanne Road.

THE UNFORTUNATE JONES, OR DEATH AT THE FINAL

A Family Story

MY GRANDFATHER RICHARD JONES, and two of his brothers, William and Edward, were professional footballers in the period between the 1890s and the First World War. Not that one could live off of a footballer's wage in those days—it was not much more than beer money. A footballer had to have a day job. The brothers were from Dolgadfan, in the parish of Llanbrynmair,[1] a small community in a Welsh-speaking area of North Wales. They were the sons of tailors, Daniel and Jane Jones, who had nine children in all. There were six sons in the family and three daughters, and it was hard for them all to make ends meet in Wales. In hopes for a better life, the family left Wales sometime around 1890, and made its way to the midlands of England. The Midlands did not work out for them, so they moved again, this time to the East End of London where they settled in a tough dockland neighborhood known as The Isle of Dogs.

The daughters of Daniel and Jane Jones found work as domestics, and the sons worked as tailors or bolt makers, and three of them played football. At one time or another, Richard, William, and Edward all played for the Millwall Football Club, which had its home on the island. Thus began my family's connection to Millwall, which has continued, through thick and thin, to this day.

The club itself had been founded in 1885 by young men who came to London from around the British Isles, drawn by the opportunity to find a decent-paying job. Many came from Scotland and found work in the J. T. Morton canning factory, and it has been claimed that the factory's workers were largely instrumental in the founding of Millwall Football Club. The team's colors being the same as Scotland's national colors, blue and white, may reflect Scottish origins, or it may just be coincidence. The club, which had its first headquarters in a pub fittingly called The Islander, was founded with a noble purpose in mind: to provide an opportunity for healthy exercise for young men, and to keep them off the streets and out of the pubs.

The most useful footballer of the three brothers was Granddad Richard Jones. In addition to Millwall, he also played for Manchester City and gained international honors playing for Wales. However, this story is about Great-Uncle Will Jones and his tragic demise.

In the late 1890s, after playing for Millwall and Sheppey United, he had signed on to play for Ryde, a team on the Isle of Wight,[2] an island off of the south coast of England. The Ryde club was known as the Redshirts and played in the Hampshire league. They were a good team, and in 1899, they had a particularly fine season, reaching the final of The Isle of Wight Senior Cup tournament. They beat the team from Cowes by a score of 2–1 in the semi-final, and this set

William Jones of Ryde Football Club. The caption benath this 1898 photograph reads: "Late of Millwall and Sheppey United Football Clubs—the Clever Football Player who, while playing Sandown F.C. at Newport, on March 22nd, 1899, sacrificed his young life when shooting the winning goal and securing for his Club the Isle of Wight Senior Cup. AGED 25 YEARS.

them up to play Sandown Football club in the final. Sandown, sometimes called The Bay Boys, was said to have a "rough crowd," and there was tension between the supporters. A Sandown supporter was most direct when he said that all the Ryde team was fit for was to be "cut up for bait for his lobster pots." He added that he would like to do the job himself. Not a good start. Ryde supporters gave as good as they got, and insults were freely hurled from both sides.

Match day was the March 22, 1899, and the game was to be played at a neutral ground in a district of Newport known as Church Litten.[3] It was a sellout, and according to newspaper accounts it was an exciting and close game that was tied at two goals each until the closing minutes. With the referee looking at his watch and getting ready to blow the final whistle, Great-Uncle Will received the ball and made a lighting run for the goal. The Sandown goalkeeper, Robert Reed, came out of his goal to narrow the angle, and the inevitable happened—they collided. At the moment of contact, Uncle Will slid the ball past the Sandown keeper and scored what was to be the winning goal.

At the inquest,[4] one of the witnesses said the shot was "a regular daisy cutter." Both players were knocked to the ground by the force of the collision. Goalkeeper Reed got up, but Great-Uncle Will did not. Stretcher bearers came onto the field along with two doctors, Preston and Mackenzie, who were at the game. They went directly to Uncle Will and found that he was conscious but in great pain. He was asking to be taken away.

It was soon apparent that he was badly injured and was fading fast. He was carried off the field, put on a St. Johns Ambulance wheeled stretcher, and pushed on a horrendous journey of ten miles over rough bumpy tracks from Church Litten to Ryde Infirmary. The bearers stopped at the Sloop Inn[5] at Wooton Bridge to refresh themselves and administer hot brandy to Uncle Will. They did finally get him to the infirmary, where he spent the night and most of the next day in great distress. The early diagnosis of his injuries was broken ribs and "concussion of the heart." Reed, the Sandown goalkeeper and a good sporting fellow, came to see him, but Uncle Will was already too far gone to talk. A report said, "The poor fellow gradually sank, till shortly before midnight on Thursday, he passed away." One is left to wonder if he might have survived without the hot brandy and the ordeal of the journey to the infirmary.

There was a strange twist; it was said at the inquest that, "On poor Jones, when undressed, was found a letter from his sister, imploring him to give up playing football." He had three sisters, and it is unknown which wrote the letter, but what had happened to make her write it, and why was Uncle Will carrying it with him?

The inquest, to determine if anyone was at fault, focused on the actions of goalkeeper Reed. Many witnesses testified, including the referee, attending doctors, and some spectators. The Ryde team captain, Frank Mozart Walker (whose parents may have hoped that he would pursue a different career), also testified. The determination of the jury was that the keeper could not be blamed, as he was going for the ball and not the player. They expressed deep sympathy for the family and friends of "the poor young fellow" who had met with such a melancholy end. The verdict was accidental death, but the jury added a "strong rider" that said that power should be given to referees to prevent rough play. Maybe the very rough play in those days was the reason for the letter from Will's sister. It was determined by the splendidly named Dr. Augustus Kissey Morgan, house surgeon at the infirmary, that Uncle Will died from a ruptured intestine.

The Isle of Wight Football Association, at the suggestion of its chairman, The Rev. P. G. U. Pickering, sent condolences to the sister of the "young fellow Jones," whose sad death they all deplored, and to the young lady to whom he was so shortly to be married. They also sent sympathies to Robert Reed for the insults he had been receiving from the Ryde supporters. Reed, who had injured a finger in the collision, thanked the Football Association and passed on the reassuring news that his finger was on the mend. Who was the "young lady" that Great Uncle Will was to marry? We will never know for sure, but among the mourners, and with the brothers and sisters of Uncle Will, was a Miss Wheeler. Was it she who was Uncle Will's intended? It will forever remain an aching mystery.

On the day set for the interment of Uncle Will, the town of Ryde was brought to a standstill. Shops were closed and shuttered, and window blinds drawn. The *County Press* wrote that Holy Trinity church in Ryde was packed with mourners, and further declared, "The whole town, practically the whole Island attended." The coffin was borne from Uncle Will's lodgings to the church for the funeral service. Enormous crowds lined the streets to see the procession go by. The "remains" of Great-Uncle Will, who was referred to in the *Island Newspapers* as the *The Unfortunate Jones,* were laid in a fine coffin of polished elm with brass fittings. The inscription on the coffin read: *William Jones, died March 23rd, 1899, aged 25 years.*

At one time, Uncle Will had been a member of the Holy Trinity Church Choir, so the choir claimed the privilege of giving him a choral funeral. As the coffin was being carried into the church, the organist, Mr. Percy James, played "O Rest in the Lord." The hymn "When Our Heads Are Bowed with Woe" was sung, and "Psalm 39" was chanted. Then the vicar gave quite a flowery eulogy. Finally, the congregation sang "Abide with Me," after which, "The Dead March" was played. The coffin, bedecked with flowers, was taken from the church by eight Redshirt players and placed on a horse-drawn carriage to be taken through the streets of Ryde, to the grave-yard. His brothers and sisters were in following carriages, along with his landlady and the mysterious Miss Wheeler. By all accounts it was a grand funeral, and probably would have been quite bewildering to Great-Uncle Will had he been an observer. The address by the vicar was a bit over the top but was very good. He spoke of a "a life so bright in itself and so fertile in brightness to others." Well, it was in the time of Queen Victoria. However, he did make reference to an Italian archbishop who had been held in high regard for three hundred years for his service to the poor at the time of the great plague. The archbishop had been asked by a friend what he would do if the last trumpet were to sound and find him engaged in a game of billiards. He replied that he would try to make the next stroke as good as possible.

I doubt that Great-Uncle Will heard any trumpets, but there is no doubt that his last kick of the football was as good a kick as he could possibly have made.

THERE IS A POSTSCRIPT. To be eligible to play for Ryde, a player had to live within five miles of the ground or have lived on the Isle of Wight for twenty-eight days. Someone from the Sandown Club decided to find out just how far away the Ryde players lived. They found, or claimed to have found, that two of the Ryde players were living in Portsmouth, which is on the south coast of England. Sandown Football Club, via none other than their captain, Goalkeeper Robert Reed, then filed a protest with the league to have the result of the match overturned. Not content with doing away with Great-Uncle Will, they wanted the cup as well. The Football Association called a meeting to investigate the matter, but in a gesture of magnificent contempt, Ryde refused to attend the meeting and said that, under the circumstances, they preferred that Sandown should win under protest "what they could not win in a game." Chagrinned, the Bay Boys backed down and said that they did not want to win the cup that way.

A report from that time claims that, due to the controversy, the cup was not awarded to either side, and no medals were given to the players. However, the inscription under the memorial photograph at the beginning of this story says that William Jones, "sacrificed his young life when shooting the winning goal and securing for his club the Isle of Wight Senior Cup." That's good enough for me; the result of the match still stands, and Uncle Will did score a historic and brilliant goal.

The newspapers said that, in his death, there passed away the finest outside right playing in Hampshire. I don't know how well endowed with outside rights Hampshire was in 1899, but it is equally nice to know that Great-Uncle Will was considered by some to have been the best of them.

The Jones family can hope, but never expect, to have such a funeral for one of its own again, but you never know. A fine tombstone for Great-Uncle Will stands today in the Ryde cemetery. Engraved on it are these words: *This memorial is erected by the members and supporters of the Ryde Football Club as a token of their appreciation of his many brilliant and faithful services.* On looking at it, using the terminology of today's young folk, one might be tempted to say: "Way to go, Uncle Will."

Endnotes

1. The original settlers of Venedocia, Ohio, came from farms near to Llanbrynmair. In English, Llanbrynmair means "Saint Mary's on the Hill."

2. The Isle of Wight is England's largest island. It lies about five miles off of the south England. Newport is its capital. Some famous full- and part-time residents of the Isle of Wight include Queen Victoria; Charles Dickens; Alfred Noyes, poet, who wrote "The Highwayman"; and Cardell "Scum" Goodman, seventeenth-century actor, murderer, Jacobite, and highwayman. King Charles I was imprisoned on the island in 1648. He tried to escape by climbing out of a window but got stuck between the bars.

3. Church Litten. A part of Newport. "Litten" is from a Saxon word meaning "cemetery."

4. Report of the Coroners Inquest and of the funeral, printed in the *Isle of Wight Observer* on March 25 and April 1, 1899.

5. The Sloop Inn at Wooton Bridge still stands.

THOMAS GREY
AND MR. LEGGET

A Reminiscence of London School Life

WORLD WAR II ENDED IN MID-1945, and I returned to London. My life as an evacuee in the country was over. As I noted in a previous tale, I had failed my eleven-plus examination, and with that failure went my chances of going to a grammar school. Instead, I was placed in a secondary school named Colls Road, a large Victorian pile of bricks in Peckham. It was named Colls Road because that was the name of the road it was built on, and that is the way secondary schools were named. It was a state school, which means it was under the control of a government department, the Ministry of Education. In addition to grammar and secondary schools, there were, and still are, public schools. That sounds all right—one might think they were for everyone—but, in fact, public schools are actually very expensive, and exclusive, private schools. This is quite confusing to those who were not brought up in England, and even to those who were.

Colls Road school was for boys and girls aged eleven to fifteen, and the requirement to get in was not very high. Failing the eleven plus examination would do it. I don't know why it was called the eleven-plus, because it was often taken sometime before a student reached eleven years old. The intent of the exam was to separate those considered capable of benefiting from a higher academic education from those who the examiners thought would be better off with a more functional education. Secondary school, however, did provide a broad and solid program of studies that would enable students to get by in the working world.

Generally, the boys' studies had a technical bent (they did metalwork, woodwork, and technical drawing), while the program for girls leaned more toward commercial skills and how to keep house. There was a class called "Home Economics," which was basically about how to shop and cook. It was for girls only. Knowing how to shop and cook are useful skills for everyone, but the expected roles for girls and for boys were firmly set, and there was no need for boys to know anything about cooking.

Boys and girls all wore school uniforms—a dark jacket with a badge on the breast pocket, and a school tie. I have always liked school uniforms; they look smart, and I think they help to give students an identity.

I stayed at the school until a few months short of my sixteenth birthday, then left to find a job for a couple of years until I would face the Military Draft Board at the age of eighteen. The probability was that I would be drafted into the army.

When I did face the board, I failed the medical exam. To that point, I was doing quite well at failing things. It was a great disappointment to me, as I had looked forward to getting on a regimental boxing team if I got into the army. Friends had told me that the army saw to it that you got more and better food if you were a boxer, but thinking about it later, I doubted that was true.

My brother did his two years of National Service with the Gloucestershire regiment, known as the "Glorious Gloucesters." He seemed to have had an interesting and enjoyable experience, spending much of his service around Montego Bay, in the sunny climes of Jamaica.

There was no school-leaving certificate at the end of the four or five years of schooling, nothing to show to a potential employer what a student had accomplished. A female job placement officer came to the school to give advice on how to find a reasonable line of work that did not require too much in the way of academic achievements in mathematics, science, and so on. She did talk about apprenticeships to various trades, or maybe being a car mechanic, all good and useful jobs, but never was the benefit of going to night school to earn a School Leaving Certificate mentioned. We had "failed," and that was that. My idea at the time was to join the Royal Navy. My Uncle Alf had been in the navy, and it sounded like a grand life.

Were the four or five years I spent at Colls Road School all a waste of time? Some of it was, but there were some silver linings, and the quality of the education we did get was good.

We studied history, which I liked, although much of it was about the Soviet Union and the glory of its five-year plans. Some of the teachers were quite left-wing and thought that Joe Stalin was a good guy. He was often called Uncle Joe. We also read great books and acted in classic plays. Shakespeare and Dickens were the most popular authors chosen by the teachers. I was an enthusiastic actor, and, wrapped in a bed sheet loaned from my mother, I played the part of

Marc Antony to what I thought was great effect, in *Julius Caesar;* I was Quince in *A Midsummer Night's Dream,* while a girl named Ann White was a dazzling Titania. I was totally overwhelmed by Ann White. I tried to think of clever things to say to her but always stumbled and said something that was not clever at all. Other theatrical roles included me being an unconvincing Fagin in *Oliver Twist.* In class, we read Sir Walter Scott's *Ivanhoe.* It was a big hit. That was some years before the movie, in which Robert Taylor as Ivanhoe finishes up with Joan Fontaine instead of Elizabeth Taylor—a baffling choice. There were bible studies twice a week, led by the gym teacher, and choral singing led by whichever teacher could play the piano. The songbook used in English schools at that time included wonderful folk songs collected by Cecil Sharp and the Reverend S. Baring Gould, so, in general, the songs were good. The more classical songs like "Who is Sylvia" and "Nymphs and Shepherds" did not fit so well with school children in the east end of London, whereas "The Lincolnshire Poacher" and "The Golden Vanity" did. I, along with some others in my class, did get to sing with the London Schools Children's Choir at the famous Guild Hall near to Westminster Abbey. I'm not sure how we were selected for this— we were OK boy sopranos, but far from the best.

Every morning, there was a full school assembly where announcements were made, prayers said, and hymns sung. There was always a sermon from the headmaster, which he had supposedly written himself, then after a closing hymn, we were dismissed to go back to our classrooms.

A couple of times a year, my class was taken up to the West End of London to see something special. I remember enjoying the opera "The Marriage of Figaro" and the play "The Admirable Chricton" by J. M. Barrie. The latter made a big impression on me. Chricton is pronounced without the middle "c," so one wonders as to why it is there. The story is about a very wealthy upper-class family that, along with their man servant, Chricton, gets shipwrecked on a deserted island. It turns out that Chricton is the only one in the party with any sense of what is practical, and who knows what it will take to survive. So he becomes the leader and exercises stern, sensible, and absolute rule. The rich family obeys his every word; then, sadly for Chricton, a ship appears on the horizon, and they are all rescued. Chricton reverts to being a manservant, and they all go home, returning to the pre-shipwreck order of running things, with the rich folks oblivious of what they owed to their admirable manservant. A very unfair ending, I thought at the time, but that is the way it would have ended in real life.

On the walls of most English classrooms at that time hung a map of the world. Large sections of the map were colored in pink, to designate the countries that were a part of the British Empire. The pink seemed to have covered about a third of the planet. We were taught that the empire was a very good thing, and that the indigenous people who lived in the countries ruled by Britain were very grateful and loved the Royal Family. We were not told of the hundreds of thousands of men from India, the African colonies, and others from far-flung bits of the empire who were drafted to fight and die in European wars that had nothing to do with them.

Maps of London in the 1950s showed a swath of green all around London called the Green Belt. It was land intended to be easily accessible countryside for Londoners. We, and all Londoners, were told that the Green Belt was sacrosanct and would never be developed beyond the roads that went through it. No factories, houses, or major roads would be allowed to invade this green paradise. However, with population growth and more and more people owning cars, "progress" required a massive ring road around London, and more houses, so we got the M25. Then more houses and urban expansion followed. The Green Belt was losing the battle.

Competitive sports were encouraged in schools in those postwar years, and at Colls Road we had opportunities for games. We did not have our own playing field, but there were local sports grounds we could use for football and cricket, and there was a fine running track in Deptford Park, not too far away. I did well at boxing and swimming and won championships in Deptford, Greenwich, and Camberwell in both sports, and one London championship in swimming, while I was outrageously robbed of another. One can see the sad tale under the heading of "Two Great Swimming Disasters." I only made reserve for the football team, however, and was never chosen to play cricket, although I did join a cricket club when I left school.

I enjoyed woodwork and metal work classes. We learned how to use a lathe and how to temper steel. Sticking a piece of metal into a white-hot furnace and then pounding it with a hammer is something that would please any schoolboy. I still have a fine table that I made in woodwork class.

Then there were school journeys. These would take us across the channel by boat to France, Belgium, and Holland. When in those countries, we tramped through many famous museums, hauling our satchels, stuffed with bottles of lemonade and sticky buns. The teachers hoped, mostly in vain, that their students would acquire some appreciation of art and the finer things in life. Maybe a thing or two did rub off here and there. I vividly remember, while in Holland, seeing the Rembrandt masterpiece *The Changing of the Nightwatch*. It was so powerful that I never forgot it. It looked as though the watchmen were about to step out of the painting and into the room to be among us. Also, while in Holland, we played some local lads at football and were badly beaten. We put it down to home field advantage. With all of this exposure to culture and the master painters of Europe, we were ready for art class at Colls Road School.

That class was taught by Mr. Legget, a stern and heavily built man with a wooden leg. He was about sixty years old and a veteran of the First World War, he sported very small horn-rimmed glasses and wore heavy three-piece brown tweed suits. He taught conventional art classes, which I enjoyed, but his passion was for calligraphy, the art of beautiful writing, using a broad tipped pen with strong strokes down and light strokes up. Learning and practicing calligraphy were mandatory in Mr. Legget's class.

At times, he would leave the blackboard and stand by the window, gazing out over the roofs and sooty chimney pots of the houses on Colls Road. He seemed to have drifted into another place and time. He would talk, slowly, about that terrible war, the war that was supposed to end all wars. He talked more, it seemed, to himself than to us, his students, but we listened intently. He spoke of a horse-drawn gun carriage stuck in the mud, and he, along with other soldiers, his mates, trying to force that gun carriage forward. They pushed, pulled, slipped, fell in the mud, and screamed at the poor horses. They beat them and urged them to pull. Horse and man were exposed to bullets, exploding shells, and flying shrapnel, and they were stuck in the mud, the inescapable mud of Flanders. It was in such an action that one of Mr. Legget's legs was blown off. The army replaced it with the wooden leg, so of course the name he got from callous schoolboys was Pegleg Legget. Today, knowing so much more about the horrors of the First World War, and what those soldiers and horses went through, maybe we would show more respect. I certainly hope that we would. We should have known better, as so many homes had a picture on the wall, usually over the fireplace, of a relative who did not come home from that conflict. In my family, we had Great-Uncle Rueben Skeels, killed in action in 1917 and buried in *Dickebusch* Military Cemetery in Belgium. Many years later, when I was more than seventy-five years old, I visited his grave. It was strangely moving to stand at the grave site and read the inscription on the gravestone of someone I never knew but had heard about since childhood. Here he was, my great-uncle

Reuben Skeels of the East Surrey Regiment. Killed in action in 1917, he was buried in a military cemetery in Belgium

Rueben, forever twenty-five years old. I have a picture of him as a young man in his soldier's uniform, wearing his army hat and with bandoliers of bullets around his neck. It hangs on a wall in our house today.

Mr. Legget was a disciplinarian, but unlike some other teachers and the very severe headmaster, he did not resort to using the cane. Poor behavior in class brought a form of punishment that had some educational value. He would direct an offending pupil to "write out ten ten-letter words, ten times each." Thank goodness it was not required that the words be written out in a student's best attempt at calligraphy. Finding words with ten letters in them was bad enough.

Mr. Legget prepared the certificates to be awarded to school-children for academic and sporting achievements; I have some of those for boxing and swimming, and a couple on the academic front.

Calligraphy practice was intense, but there was some relief if you were printing out something you liked. At that time, I liked the 1750 poem "Elegy Written in a Country Churchyard," by Thomas Grey. It is a long poem about dead people, and many of the verses, it seemed to me, were repetitive but beautifully written. The poem tells us that the lives of the common folk were worthwhile, and muses on the unfulfilled potential that may have lain within each of them. It contains the famous line: "The paths of glory lead but to the grave." It is said that, before the Battle of Quebec in 1759, the commander of the British and American Army, General Wolfe, declared, "Gentlemen, I would rather have written that poem than take Quebec tomorrow." A bit over the top on the part of the general, perhaps—after all, his job was to win battles. But back to my calligraphy: I selected a verse, a good one I think, that sums up the essence of the poem. This was my chosen verse and attempt at calligraphy:

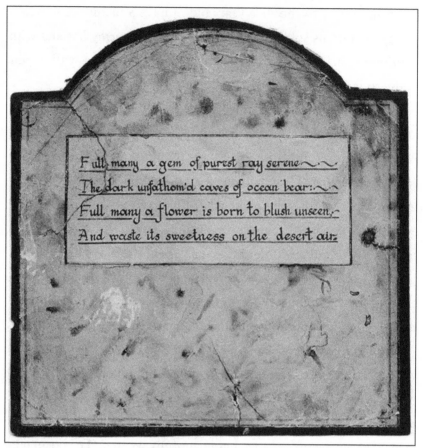

Full many a gem of purest ray serene
The dark unfathom'd caves of ocean bear:
Full many a flower is born to blush unseen,
And waste its sweetness on the desert air.

My calligraphic venture

Some in the class came up with very good efforts at illuminated texts. Not quite the *Book of Kells*, maybe, but those old monks of long ago had to start somewhere.

Colls Road School did what the educators had intended for it and others like it. It gave boys and girls enough skills to get some sort of job and to earn a living, but it did not prepare students for a higher education and so lay down a pathway to professional careers. It had been decided by an academic measure, when a boy or girl was ten years old, what their futures should hold. The system underwent some changes in the 1970s that gave late bloomers a second chance, but that was too late for me. Later, I did go to night school and got some diplomas and professional qualifications.

Some of the teachers were good; one or two were very good and took their responsibilities to educate their charges seriously. Others were mediocre at best. One, Mr. Wilson, was very good and I liked him, but he made the fatal mistake of depending on the better nature of fourteen-year-old boys. When things were getting rough in the classroom, he would try appealing to their better nature, telling them that the job he had was his "bread and butter." This was like fresh bait to some boys, and one of them threw an ink dart at Wilson as he was writing on the blackboard, staining his jacket. Mr. Wilson turned round in anger and cursed the boy with what today would be considered a very mild curse word. The boy's mother got to hear of this, and she complained to the headmaster. Mr. Wilson was fired. What the poor man did after that, I don't know, and the headmaster shrank in my eyes: He should have stood up for Mr. Wilson. Some, including the headmaster, made more use of the cane on boys than was necessary; the girls were never caned. Then, once in a while, a teacher, maybe a most unlikely one, would offer something different and set a young boy or girl thinking and give them something they would remember for life. I think it is fair to say that the unlikely Mr. Legget was such a teacher, and he did open a door that, hopefully, some of his students chose to pass through.

TWO SWIMMING DISASTERS

School Days And Swimming Races

Disaster One: The Oversized Swimming Trunks

BRIAN FAIRHURST WAS FROM YORKSHIRE, a fine county in the North of England. In the late 1940s, he was in my class at Colls Road School. He was the only non-Londoner in our class, probably in the whole school, and he seemed so different from the rest of us that he could have come from Mars. He was a bit shorter than average, had red hair, and was somewhat thick around the middle, but it was his strong Yorkshire accent that set him apart. The rest of us were South East Londoners, and most of us spoke in Cockney accents.

When I was going to school, sports were very popular, especially swimming; it was part of the school curriculum, and we had to learn all of the strokes and also practice life-saving drills. When a certain standard was reached, certificates or medals were awarded. I still have many of mine. The certificate for swimming fifty yards is magnificent; it is adorned with waves, dolphins and mermaids. I don't think you get many mermaids on certificates today. The life-saving medals, however, are somewhat dubious. Life-saving, as taught to London school children in the 1940s, was predicated on the assumption that the drowning person would be entirely passive and would cooperate. He, or she, would greet the would-be rescuer with calm and a reasonable attitude, and follow the instructions given by the heroic lifesaver. One drill was to persuade the distressed swimmer to take a floating, face-up position in the water and to place his or her hands on the shoulders of the rescuer who, swimming the breast stroke, would push the unfortunate victim to safety. This didn't sound very practical to us even then, but we practiced it anyway.

To prepare for races, we swam laps a couple of times a week at the spectacular Laurie Grove Baths in Deptford. The Jacobean-style building that housed the baths had been constructed under the Public Baths and Wash-House Act of 1846. Who would ever have thought that Parliament passed something called The Public Baths and Wash-House Act? But it was a great thing that they did. These "all-purpose" baths enabled anyone to go for a swim, or a bath, hot or cold, and to take their laundry with them. The laundry would be washed but not dried. On the next day, the damp laundry could be picked up and taken home in a bag to be hung out to dry. It was known as "The Bagwash." A useful excuse for being late for school was to say to the teacher, "I had to go to the Bagwash for me mum." ("Me" was more commonly used than "My.")

Getting back to the swimming, when I say "prepare for races," I have to add that it wasn't too strenuous. Our swimming "coach," Mr. Green, a thin, bent-over man whom no one had ever seen in the swimming pool, would have us swim up and down the pool a few times and then kick our feet in the water while hanging on to the side of the pool. We didn't do the racing turns that they do nowadays, where they don't even touch the end of the pool with their hands—that would have been considered cheating; we just touched the wall with a hand, turned round, and pushed off.

I had quite good form in all of the strokes, so Mr. Green would call on me and say, "Show us the backstroke, Jonesey." I would swim a length while the other boys watched. They were supposed to pick up style points, but they were not impressed and they were not slow in letting me know it—they gave me a hard time for getting in a bit more swimming than they did. I did swim laps on my own in the Peckham Health Center pool. The Center, a magnificent building near to where I lived, housed a twenty-five-yard pool and diving boards that met Olympic requirements. In 1948 the British Olympic swimmers and divers trained at the Center. The British team coach was there, and he gave us young folks some racing tips.

The local school swim meets for the Deptford and Greenwich Championships were held at the Laurie Grove pool, and winners went on to compete in the London championships at the Marshall Street Baths in Westminster, which were very famous at the time (many championship events took place there). My best strokes were the breaststroke and the backstroke, and I came first in the Deptford and Greenwich backstroke race several times and was outrageously robbed of a London championship in that stroke, but that's another story. I also swam for the school in relay races and, one year, we did win the London championship in the Butterfly relay race.

In 1949, I was to swim for my school in the free-style relay race for the championship of Deptford and Greenwich: four boys in each team. We stood a good chance of winning and were all very confident of victory. My great misfortune on that day was to turn up at the Laurie Grove pool only to find that I had forgotten to bring my swimming trunks with me, which was a problem, and a bad mistake. Actually, it was a bit more than that, it was a disaster. It was much too late to go home and get my trunks, so I scouted around to see if I could borrow a pair. I asked every boy of approximately my size if I could borrow his; none of them wanted to lend them to me. Maybe they knew that, without trunks, I could not swim in the race, so the Colls Road team would have to withdraw. It was not looking good—and then I saw Brian Fairhurst. He was not there to swim in the races; he had come along to watch and then take a dip when the racing was over. I said, "Brian, can I borrow your swimming trunks?" Brian said it was OK with him and gave them to me. I went into the dressing room to change and put the trunks on. They fit, alright, maybe not as snug as my own trunks, but I didn't think much about it.

I came out to the pool ready to race. Nowadays, they do warm-ups before racing, but in those days we didn't bother with warm-ups; it was just dive in and swim as fast as you could. It would have been so much better for me if we had had warm-ups.

The galleries, which were along each side, and above, the pool, were packed with mums and dads and screaming boys and girls. They looked directly down on the pool and the swimmers. Sadly for me, there were lots of girls—very loud and very enthusiastic girls, who gave great support to swimmers from their own schools and outright abuse to swimmers from other schools.

The race was four times fifty yards, and as the pool was twenty-five yards long, all four of us started from the same end. I think I was number three, and we were in a good position when my turn came, in fact we were narrowly in the lead. I stood at the pool's edge, waiting for my teammate to touch the end of the pool, and when he did, I made my best Olympic style racing dive, and as I entered the water, I felt something around my ankles. . .Brian Fairhurst's swimming trunks! The galleries exploded with laughter, there were delighted shrieks and vulgar shouts from the girls; this was, after all, the East End of London. I had to tread water while I pulled up Brian's oversized trunks, I then bravely swam the first length. At the turn, I was half prepared for disaster when I pushed off from the pool wall, and managed to grab the trunks before they reached my knees, but the girls in the galleries were waiting and they let out more screams and hoots. I swam the length to finish my leg and sheepishly, and very carefully, pulled myself out of the pool. Hearing the derisive laughter from the spectators and feeling that I had let my teammates down, I tried to disappear as quickly as possible. Needless to say, we did not win the race, didn't even place, but as a small consolation, we were not last.

I was very embarrassed and felt I should make an apology to Mr. Green for our team not winning; the best I could come up with was, "Sir, my swimming trunks came down." "I know Jonesey," he said, "I know."

Disaster Two: Robbed

A far more painful experience than the Oversized Swimming Trunks Disaster came in the 1950 final of the London Schools Senior Boys Backstroke. This was for boys around fifteen years old. The venue was the historic and majestic, Marshall Street Baths in Westminster, which, like the Laurie Grove Baths had its beginning under the Public Baths and Wash-House Act, some time in the 1850s. At its birth it had similar facilities to the baths at Laurie Grove, a swimming pool, a laundry complete with cubicles for ironing, and hot baths. There were also cold baths at half the price of the hot ones. In addition there was a day care center, and many more conveniences for the citizens of Westminster. A major renovation of the building took place in the late 1920s which resulted in the magnificent facility that hosted the 1950 London Schools Swimming Championship.

The pool only had six racing lanes, but it was a masterpiece of design and construction. There was much decoration and ornamentation, bronze fountains, statues of dolphins stood in niches in the walls and the pool glistened with marble, Sicilian white and Swedish green. The glorious barrel-vaulted roof had many skylights that allowed natural light to flood the pool during daylight hours, well, that is most of the daylight hours.

In the 1940s, London was notorious for thick, noxious fogs. They were called "Peasoupers." At times it was barely possible to see your hand in front of your face.

I may have been overwhelmed by the surroundings, but I was probably so full of nerves over the upcoming race, that I had no time to admire the architecture. I had to get myself ready to race for the championship of London. My usual way of preparing for any race, be it running or swimming, was to lie down on my back and try not to move a muscle. I thought this would conserve energy and I would do this until race time. None of us young swimmers had been taught, or coached, in the benefits of "warming up". Today, anyone who is about to race will swim many laps at varying speeds before racing.

The pool was three lengths for 100 yards. Not long enough for international racing, although Johnny Weissmuller, the first and most famous of the movie Tarzan's, and a five-time Olympic Gold medalist, had swum there. He was by far, the fastest swimmer of his day.

My race was to be a sprint. I had won my heats and the semi final, so I had a good shot at becoming the London champion. The racers were called out to the pool and told to take starting places. Lanes were not assigned, swimmers took their choice, and for some reason, I chose to swim in an outside lane, right up against the pool wall. Nowadays, the center lanes are considered to have "faster water", so swimmers are assigned lanes based on their times in the heats. Had any of us known this, there would have been quite a scramble for the center lanes. My rational for choosing the outside lane was that by turning my head to the left, I would be able to see all of the other swimmers. As it turned out, my rational made no sense at all.

Compared to today, there was a very casual approach to school swimming competitions, there was no regular disciplined training to speak of, and what there was is described in the story of the great swimming trunks disaster. Some laps at Laurie Grove Swimming Pool and a few more at the Peckham Health Center did it for me. However, most of us did some athletic training and gym work.

We were called to our marks then the gun went off. I got a very good start and swam well to finish first, well ahead of the second-place finisher. I was feeling great and was celebrating. A winner would go to a ceremony at the mighty Guild Hall in London. Just across from Westminster Abbey, and be given a fine silver cup. You could only keep the cup for a year of course, and it would be kept at the school, but a winner's name would be engraved on it. Visions of that cup were going through my head when through noise and my water filled ears, I heard a woman's raspy voice screaming at me. It was the voice of Miss Wood, one of my teachers. "Touch the wall" she yelled. I didn't know what she was talking about. "Touch the wall", she yelled again, 'you only touched the ladder, you must touch the end of the pool." A wooden ladder that took up half the width of the lane, had been left in the corner of the pool. Swimming backwards made it impossible for me to see it. I just brought my right arm over for the last stroke and my hand landed on the ladder. By the time I touched the wall two other swimmers had come in.

I was dumbfounded and confused. I protested first to Miss Wood, but she would have none of it. My protests were probably incoherent, and I was ignored, except by spectators who sat right across from the finish line. "HE WON, HE WON," they shouted. One spectator pointed at me and shouted directly at the judges to let them know that I had won the race. I tried to approach the judges table but was curtly dismissed. A re-race would not be considered and I had been disqualified for touching the ladder.

I got no support from Miss Wood, a scrawny and wrinkled Wicked Witch of the West type woman, or from our so called swimming coach, Mr. Green. At the school assembly on the following morning, when Mr. Green gave a report on the performances of our team, he spent a long time talking about one of our swimmers who had won the senior boys 100 yards race. Ernie Nye was his name. Without any doubt at all, Ernie was our schools best swimmer, he was a natural and cleaved through the water like a hot knife through butter. I more hoped than expected that Mr. Green would make some mention of my race, and of the controversial finish. My hopes were dashed, Mr. Green had nothing to say. After all these years, the taste is still bitter. It is an unhappy memory.

The London Schools Finals were the pinnacle of swimming for any boy or girl swimmer. It was tough to be so blatantly robbed, and without the support of a teacher there was little recourse for an appeal, but in later years I wished that I had at least tried. I could have approached the judges and asked them to explain how I could be expected to see the ladder while swimming backwards. That would have floored them, what could they say? I could have asked them why wasn't the ladder removed from the pool to make for a clear racing lane. There was a whole slew of brilliant and logical arguments I could have made, but I didn't. At fourteen years old one does not think of coherent arguments, and even if one did, school boys and girls were not allowed to challenge a teacher, you just had to accept that they knew best, even though you knew that they didn't. So there you go. What I did do was to look hopelessly for help, but with the exception of the spectators on the finish line who shouted "HE WON," no help came. Not even from Mr. Green. My only consolation was that at least, my swimming trunks stayed up.

I general, I have good memories of school swimming meets, especially of my team mates. With reservations, I do not think badly of Mr. Green. As for Miss Wood, however, well I really can't say, but I do know what happened to the Wicked Witch of the West.

SMITH OF LAMBETH

A Schoolboy Boxer

IN THE LATE 1940s, I WAS on the boxing team for my school in Peckham, South East London. I was fanatical about everything to do with boxing. I collected sets of cigarette cards of boxers, cut out pictures of fighters from the newspapers, and listened to radio broadcasts of the big fights. I was in the fish-and-chips shop at the corner of Nunhead Green on the night that Randolph Turpin defeated the great Sugar Ray Robinson for the world middleweight title. The date was July 10, 1951, a celebrated date in British boxing history. The shop owner had the radio on, so I stayed to listen to the round-by-round commentary. The fight went the full fifteen rounds, so there I stood, holding my soggy fish and chips for a full hour. Along with many others, I went home surprised and elated when Turpin got the decision.

I was very excited by Britain's post-war boxing champions, especially a Yorkshireman named Bruce Woodcock, who was at his peak in the late 1940s. The experts told us he had a good shot at being the heavyweight champion of the world. Britain had a long history of horizontal heavyweights, but it looked as though boxing fans might at last be getting a break with Bruce. After he had done away with the European heavyweights of the late 1940s and had won the European Championship, his managers got overly ambitious. In April 1947, they put him up against an American fighter whom no one in Britain had ever heard of. His name was Joe Baksi, a former coal miner from Pennsylvania, and he was enormous. The fight almost ended in the first round when Joe broke the jaw of our hero Bruce and knocked him down multiple times. It was soon over, but that did not deter Woodcock's managers, who put him in the ring with another American named Lee Savold. Bruce was badly beaten again. His incompetent managers had overreached and pushed him too quickly. The result was not surprising, but it was devastating. I had pinned great hopes on Bruce Woodcock becoming the world's heavyweight champion, but it was not to be.

But back to my schooldays. I first had to learn the art of boxing. I took lessons at the *Peckham Health Center,* an amazing facility one block from my family's house. The trainer was a former professional heavyweight named Jack Petkin. He was assisted by his friend, Mike Mancini. Mike looked a lot like the mafia guy Clemenza in the *Godfather* movies and was from a boxing family. His brother Alf had been a middleweight contender in the 1930s, and his nephew, Tony, fought for the British lightweight title in the 1950s. Jack Petkin and Mike Mancini taught me how to slip punches, throw double left hooks, and execute the all-important straight left. When I had a boxing match, usually in South East London, Mike would hire a limousine to take Jack Petkin, my dad, me, and a few of Mike's mates to the venue. He often ordered fish and chips, wrapped in newspaper, to eat in the car. The newspaper of choice to wrap around fish and chips in those days was *News of the World*, a popular scandal sheet.

I must have been the only fifteen-year-old amateur boxer in London to be taken to the venue in a limousine. I did have some ability but lacked a real fighting spirit, or the will, to be a true winner. I enjoyed the training and the sparring but did not enjoy the boxing tournaments. I suffered severely from nerves.

At Colls Road School, the gym teacher, Mr. Green, who also taught French and swimming, was in charge of the boxing team. As I have mentioned, he was bent forward at the waist so that the top half of his body was always at about a twenty-degree angle from the vertical— not your standard gym teacher. His job was to see to it that the boxers were fit and well-schooled in boxing. Unlike Jack Petkin, he did not have much to offer in the way of boxing knowl-

Matt Wells—from South East London—World Welterweight Champion in 1914

edge, and no one ever saw him in the ring. He did, however, have an interesting friend—a small man with a battered face and a cauli-flower ear, named Matt Wells, a professional lightweight champion of the world at the time of the First World War. He was from the East End of London and had fought all over the world, beating many champions. At one tournament, I think it was in 1948, Wells was the honoree referee. At the end of the evening he was asked to make a short speech, and to chose the best boxer. He chose me and praised my skills, which, he said, were a fine example of scientific boxing. I was somewhat bowled over by that praise.

When the time came for the National Schoolboy Boxing Cham-pionships in 1949, I was entered in the tournament with some of my schoolmates. Our best boxer was Harry Maslin; his family sold fruit and vegetables from a barrow in Deptford High Street. Mr. Green selected the boxing team—in fact, he selected *all* the sporting teams, which was sort of strange as no one ever saw him doing any-thing sporting, but he did relate well with his students.

I didn't have a real boxing outfit, never had one until my final year of boxing, when I got real lace-up boxing boots and flashy shorts. Until that time, I wore a pair of old sneakers, shorts that my mother had made, and something like a sleeveless T-shirt. I also had a towel that I draped around my shoulders. My appearance was more likely to have elicited sympathy than to have scared any op-ponent. In the 1949 tournament, I scrambled through the first few matches and was lucky enough to win the Borough of Camberwell championship for my weight. The next round would be the semi-final for the schoolboy championship of South East London.

On the night of the championship, I went to the Flodden Road Drill Hall in Camberwell with my father, and while he went to sit

CAMBERWELL SCHOOLS AMATEUR BOXING ASSOCIATION

This is to Certify that

David Jones

of *Colls Road Secondary* School

was the Winner / ~~Runner-up~~ in the __7__ st. __10__ lb. ~~intermediate~~ ~~senior~~ class
junior

at the annual tournament held under the auspices of the above association.

signed

Date of tournament __1.3.49.__   _____ Chairman

DHWilliams. Hon. Secretary

Certificate for winning Camberwell championship

with Jack Petkin in the arena, I made my way to the dressing room to change. I put on my rather sad outfit and went to look at the notice board, to see who my opponent would be. His name was Smith, and he was the champion of Lambeth.

I knew nothing about Smith of Lambeth, so I sat in the dressing room, my towel around my shoulders, and wondered what he would be like. I knew that Lambeth was a very tough borough, famous for its Pearly King and Queen, for a dance known as the Lambeth Walk, and for its costermongers, people who sold fruit and vegetables from barrows in the street, just like my teammate Harry Maslin.

I expected to see someone in boxing attire similar to my own and was not prepared for what walked into that room—a boxer who wore real lace-up boxing boots and a black silk robe with white trim hanging open to show black silk boxing shorts. I had never seen what a real boxer might look like before.

He faced a long mirror on the wall and began a vigorous display of shadow boxing. He stamped his left foot and snorted as he threw punches, hooks, uppercuts, right crosses. He was a ferocious sight, and I sat in awe, still not aware of who this was. Then suddenly, he stopped his shadow boxing and, swiveling around to me, said in the voice of a sergeant major, "Is your name Jones?"

"Y-yes," I stammered.

"Well, I'm Smith from Lambeth, and you're boxing me," he said.

I was in total shock. I ran straight to the toilet. It could not be real, I thought, but when I emerged, very shaken, he was still there, snorting and stamping his feet. He then began to tell me about his boxing record. "Knocked out my last twelve opponents," he said. "Never hit them with my best punches, but down they went."

I fled to find Mr. Green, to make him aware of my dire situation. "Please, sir," I said, "I've got to box this kid from Lambeth. He's knocked out his last twelve opponents and says he is going to turn professional."

Mr. Green was not bothered. Why should he have been? "Don't worry about any of that, Jonesey," he said. "Show him your left, then stick your right in his dinner."

"Yes, sir", I said, sounded easy enough. By "dinner," he meant the solar plexus, that little triangle at the bottom of the rib cage.

I knew there was no escape, and I had to face the music. I made my way to the ring with my towel around my shoulders, climbed through the ropes, and sat on the stool that the second had pulled out for me. Then, Smith of Lambeth himself entered the ring; resplendent in his magnificent boxing gear, he moved around the ring, shadow boxing, jabbing, snorting, and stamping his feet, then sat down in the opposite corner. I could not take my eyes off him—he looked serenely confident while I was a bundle of nerves. My cockney second became tense and loudly sucked in his breath. "Blimey," he said, "looks like Smiff of Lamberf."

"Yes," I said, "that's right. Is he any good?"

My second heaved a sigh, paused for a few moments, patted me on the shoulder, and said, "Do your best, son."

Me—scoring with a right

The bell rang for round one. I was nervous and cautious but surprised at how easy it was to avoid Smith's punches, and I managed to land some light straight lefts toward the end of the round. My second seemed surprised that I was walking back to the corner on my own two feet but he gave me some words of encouragement. The second round was more lively, and at one point I had Smith against the ropes and landed a series of very good punches. He seemed flustered and wasn't at all the champion he had built himself up to be. At the start of the third round, I knew all I had to do was jab and move and I would win, and that is what I did. Smith never landed a punch.

I was declared the winner, and went over to the champion of Lambeth in his corner, and boldly said, "Good fight, mate."

Smith abashedly mumbled something about being weak from making the weight. I felt triumphant and thought that I had developed some fighting spirit after all.

This elation was short lived however, as in the next round of the tournament, for the championship of the whole of South London, I met Tuffin of Penge and did not fare so well. In fact, he knocked me down in the second round.

I often look back on that tournament, and on my brief boxing career; I think of the days of training and learning the boxer's art at the Peckham Health Center, with Jack Petkin and Mike Mancini. I think also of my teammate Harry Maslin and his fruit-and-veg barrow on Deptford High Street. My dad came to all of my boxing matches and training sessions. He hoped so much that I would go all the way and win the schoolboy championship of Great Britain. It is too bad that I could not do that for him, but I was not in that league.

I had boxed since the age of eleven and continued for a couple of years after leaving school, but then, when I reached eighteen and failed the medical exam for military service, I had to pack it in. I could not be a soldier or a sailor. Too bad. The doctors said there was scaring on my lungs, or something like that, and I had to give up all vigorous activity and drink three pints of milk a day. No football, boxing, or running. It was a consolation that I could play cricket, but that was all. Cricket is a lovely game, although difficult to explain to Americans. I kept up this spartan regime for two or three years; then I decided that the doctors were fatheads, so I stopped drinking milk, and I joined a boxing club, and *The Newtown* Rangers, a local football team.

Many times, over the years, I have thought of Smith of Lambeth in his fabulous boxing gear and relived that first dressing-room encounter. I sometimes have wondered whether today, in the corner of a Lambeth pub, there may sit a very aged cockney, clutching his pint, and with a faraway look in his eyes telling anyone who would listen, "You know, I once went three rounds with Jonesey of Peckham."

Endote

What Americans call soccer is called football everywhere else.

MY FRIEND SYDNEY

Y TWO CLOSEST FRIENDS AT COLLS ROAD SCHOOL were Brian Heritage and Sydney Short. We were in the same class in school—third form, I think it was. That would make us young teenagers. The three of us were members of the 1st Nunhead Salvation Army Boy Scouts Troop. Brian and I were drummers in the Scouts band, Sydney didn't play an instrument. You could be in the Scouts without being a member of the Salvation Army, as was the case for Sydney and me, and, for most of the scouts in the troop.

On Sunday mornings, our scout troop band marched around the streets of Nunhead. We marched behind the Salvation Army band, which played most of the tunes. They were a very good band. Then we would take a turn, banging on our drums and blowing our bugles, playing the five-note tunes which were all that could be managed on a bugle. We often passed by a monastery, and when we saw a monk standing at an open gate, we knew he was there to let us know that the other monks were in silent worship, so we stopped playing our instruments. The Salvation Army captain and the monk would give a friendly wave to each other as we passed by. We would stop at various locations, mostly outside pubs where the "drunkards and sinners" were to be found, and the Army captain would hold an open-air meeting in hopes of saving some of Nunhead's population from eternal damnation. He spoke fiercely of the consequences of not being "saved." Most Londoners had great respect for the Salvation Army, remembering its service during the wartime blitz. With its mobile canteens, it would be among the first to arrive at a bomb site to hand out hot tea and sandwiches to survivors and first responders.

Sydney was on the tall side and liked to box. His father had been a cook in the navy and a good amateur boxer in his day, so Sydney was taking after his dad. Brian was not a sporting type at all, while I was passionate about all competitive sports, especially swimming and boxing.

One day, Sydney did not come to school, nor did he come the next day, and then his absence stretched into weeks. He was ill. It was something to do with his heart, they said, and he was in the hospital. Brian and I went to visit him several times, we always took him some treats—oranges and chocolate—and he always looked good to us. He was alert and upbeat, and then, one day, we got word that he had been moved to another hospital. It was a different kind of hospital, we were told, a place where Sydney could rest up until he got better and was strong enough to go home and return to school. This hospital was northwest of London, in the town of Aylesbury in the county of Buckinghamshire.

It was a long way from South East London to Aylesbury, but by bus, train, and foot, Brian and I made it out there. When we visited Sydney, we always thought that he looked fine. He was always happy to see us, and with a smile on face he would be sitting up in bed, propped up by pillows. The nurses kept him in bed; they never had him seated in a chair or allowed him to walk around. It didn't seem to bother him, at least not that we could tell while we were there. He wanted Brian and me to give him news about school and the boys in our class, and about what we were doing in the scout group, anything we could tell him. He would tell us that he was feeling good and would be back in school very soon. I can't remember him ever complaining.

Then, one day, not very long after our last trip to Aylesbury, we were told by our teacher that Sydney had died. The headmaster made an announcement to the boys and girls of the school at the morning assembly, and spoke some very moving words about Sydney. The usually severe headmaster seemed genuinely distressed, and his voice trembled as he spoke and said prayers. Though Colls Road School was a state school, the morning assemblies were Church of England religious services.

Brian and I could not believe this awful news—Sydney had looked so well, and sounded so cheerful and positive, just a week or so before. How could he have died? We didn't know what to do, but after coming up with a number of thoughts and ideas, we decided that we should go to Sydney's house to see whether it was true, and whether we could talk to the parents. We all lived within a few streets of each other.

Brian and I walked to Hollydale Road, where Sydney lived and where we knew his parents would be. When we got to the house and saw that the curtains to the front windows were drawn, we got nervous; we knew what drawn curtains meant. We walked around the block, and stopped to think for a while; we needed to raise the courage to knock on the front door. Finally, we went back and nervously knocked. The door was opened by an uncle. He looked terribly sad, and in a halting voice, Brian asked him, "Is it true about Syd?"

The uncle nodded, and then closed the door. Sydney's parents were too devastated to talk to anyone.

The funeral would be a Church of England service. In those days, as is true today, church attendance by the majority of working-class Londoners was limited to baptism, marriage, and death. Folks went to other people's weddings, or funerals, or for some special event, but not much more than that. Then, when you died, off to church you would go for one last time. Most of the population was nominal Church of England, and the stock answer when asked about one's religion was C-of-E. Belief had nothing to do with it, it was just how you identified yourself. There was one Catholic boy in my class at school. He was excused from having to attend morning assembly.

Londoners were very respectful and kind towards their grieving neighbors. Workmen in the streets stopped work, stood up straight, and took their hats off when a funeral procession went by. Neighbors emerged from their houses and stood silently on the pavement to show respect for the bereaved family.

I was given the day off from school to go to Sydney's funeral. It was to be held at Nunhead Cemetery, where, at the time, many people from South East London got buried. It wasn't raining that day, but it was one of those gray and damp days so common in London. The funerals were assembly-line affairs, so Sydney's family and friends waited in line with the other funeral parties, sitting in the cars, or on the grass, for their turn at the standard service before the burial. The undertakers, who had seen it all so many times before, chatted with each other during the wait, as did some of the family members and friends. One by one, the hearses moved ahead to the door of the chapel, until finally, Sydney's turn arrived. His coffin and floral wreaths were removed from the hearse and carried into the chapel on the shoulders of the pall bearers. There, they were placed on an iron stand in the middle of the chapel. While this was happening, the mourners were ushered in to take their seats for the service. The Church of England vicar who had been appointed for the day was waiting to conduct the service, which would be his fourth? or fifth? who knew how many, funeral of the day, for someone he never knew or knew anything about. I looked around at the mourners. There were Sydney's grieving mum and dad, some of his uncles and aunts and other family members, and there were neighbors from Hollydale Road. Sydney's classroom teacher was there, and then there was me. It was a small group, and a sad scene.

The vicar droned on, telling us what a wonderful young fellow Sydney had been; how would he know, I wondered. He read from the standard text for funerals. He got to the bit about the certainty of everlasting life, and how we would all meet again in heaven, and then, from the congregation, came a piecing, heart-wrenching cry. It was Sydney's father. He shouted, "I don't believe it! How can I believe it!" and wept, and his body seemed to crumple. His head fell on his wife's shoulder, and she put her arms around him. She pulled him tight to her and embraced and comforted him with soft words. His body shook with grief for his son.

The vicar carried on with his job. After the service, I followed the small procession out into the cemetery, to Sydney's grave, where the gravediggers waited. Two ladies—I think they were neighbors—had me walk with them. They knew that I was Sydney's friend and was in need of some comfort. There were further words around the grave, "ashes to ashes" and so on, from the vicar, and then we threw lumps of earth on Sydney's coffin and watched as the gravediggers shoveled in earth until the hole was completely filled. Family and friends laid flowers on the grave, with messages to Sydney tied to them. Everyone stood around the grave for awhile, thinking their own thoughts. Sydney's parents clung to each other and sobbed. When the parents had gathered themselves together, they left the graveside to go back to their house, knowing they would never see Sydney again. They did have a younger son, who hopefully gave them some comfort. Slowly, the rest of the people left, most of them going back to join Sydney's parents' for tea and sandwiches. I walked home by myself, back to 28 Lausanne Road.

I stayed in touch with Brian Heritage, a wonderful and very genuine fellow, until we were in our early twenties. Then we went our separate ways. Brian had become a full member of the Salvation Army, and he suffered taunts from his family for this, but it did not deter him. He had ambitions of being a professional orchestra drummer and was taking serious lessons. He had a girlfriend who was as pretty as a picture in her Salvation Army lass's bonnet. She was a few years older than Brian, and sadly she was abused by Brian's family, who shouted across the street at her to "find someone your own age." She was tough and brave, however, and stood up for herself and fought back. Often, she would speak at the street corner meetings along with the Army captain, and go into the pubs to spread the word. You had to admire her—she had spirit and spoke with burning conviction. She was fearless and beautiful.

I know that Brian and his lady friend wanted to get married, but I don't know what happened. I truly hope they did marry.

Many times, our Sunday morning marches would take us from

Nunhead Green, where the Salvation Army Citadel was located, through the streets of Nunhead to Linden Grove. There, we would pass by the gates to the cemetery in which Sydney rested. Between the wrought-iron bars of the gates, we could see the long stone pathway, with trees, bushes, and gravestones on either side. The path led from the gates to the chapel where Sydney's funeral service had been held.

My friend Sydney was fourteen years old when he died.

Endnote

Nunhead Cemetery, with its fine views of the city, was one of "the magnificent seven" cemeteries of London—fifty-two acres of monuments, chapels, and the graves of the famous and the unknown. The last time I saw the cemetery, sometime in the 1970s, it had been abandoned. It was overgrown with weeds, brambles, and fallen trees. Many gravestones had collapsed and were lying on the ground, partially covered by the growth around them. It was a sad sight. For awhile, the cemetery became a nature reserve where birds and wildlife flourished until, sometime around 1980, the Friends of the Cemetery set about its restoration. It was re-opened in 2001.

NOT FORGOTTEN

Fruit Picking in East England in the 1950s and 1960s

WEST AFRICAN FOLK TALE TELLS of a warrior who went hunting for food for his family and did not return. After some time, he was given up for dead by all but his youngest child, who firmly believed that he was still alive. The child would ask each day, "Where is my father?"

Days passed into weeks, and then weeks into months, and still the warrior had not returned, and the child asked again, "Where is my father?"

The child had three older brothers who all believed that their father was dead, but finally, to placate the child, they decided to go and look for him. They went into the forest and, after some days, found a broken spear and some bones. They recognized the spear as belonging to their father.

Now these three sons had magical powers, so one son said he would assemble the bones into a skeleton, which he did; the next son put flesh on the bones; and the third son breathed life into the flesh.

The warrior then rose up and walked back to his village, where he was met with great joy and celebration. The warrior said, "I will give a fine gift to the one who has done the most to bring me back to life." Each of the three elder sons claimed to have done the most and so deserved the gift. But the warrior said, "I will give the gift to my youngest child, as this child has done the most to save me, for a man is not dead until he is forgotten."

A PLEASANT WAY FOR STUDENTS, and other folks, to earn some extra money during the summer months was to become a fruit picker. (Summer in England, by the way, is defined not by the weather, but by the calendar. It can be sunny, golden, and glorious during the months of June, July, and August, or it can rain every day. The weather forecasting folks rarely get it right.)

In England during the 1950s and into the 1980s, and in some cases even longer, there were international fruit-picking camps for students from around the world. They were run by the National Union of Students (NUS), headquartered somewhere in London. In 1954, I took myself up to the NUS office to inquire about the camps and ended up registering for one in North Cambridgeshire. The camp was located in the village of Leverington, very close to the Lincolnshire border and close to "The Wash," a very large bay on the east coast of England. It was in this bay that the notorious King John lost his treasure in 1216. The priceless treasure is said to still be there, probably deeply buried in the silt at the bottom of the bay. A golden opportunity is waiting for ambitious treasure hunters.

The camp in Leverington was very basic in its comforts, although the village did offer a good pub. The camp organizer was a brilliant Scot named Bill Murray. He was very popular with the students, and many of them, especially the young women, will remember his famous "Wakey, wakey!" call as he roused sleepy campers from their beds early in the morning. Everyone slept in bell tents set in a long, narrow field. There was a row of tents for the young women, and another row for the young men, with a ten-meter dash between the rows. A large barn became the dining hall, and a very pleasant, long wooden building was made available for evening socialization. The outside toilets were less than basic. There were only two of them and, more often than not, they were blocked. For bathing, there were a couple of rudimentary showers but no hot water. This camp would never have passed muster today, but in the 1950s we did not ask for much; many of the students had spent their young years living in occupied Europe, so they easily dealt with the few hardships. However, the cooks did a good job, and within a few days we were all in love with Leverington Camp. It was exciting to be gathered with so many young folks from different lands. I don't think I had ever seen a Swedish or a Norwegian girl before, let alone spoken to one. This was a major, eye-opening, life-changing experience.

I forget the name of the elderly farmer whose fruit we picked, but I remember it was he and his nephew who came around to the camp on Fridays to give us our wages. They were very fair to the students, sometimes even paying them a bit extra.

While picking strawberries in the month of June, I found myself in a row next to a beautiful Norwegian girl named Aud. We talked and talked, and our picking got slower and slower. Aud was the first person to tell me about the great Norwegian playwright Henrik Ibsen. I could not believe that he was as good as she said he was, but some fifty years later I appeared in two of his plays in New York

City, *Rosmelholm* and *The Master Builder.* Aud was right; he was a genius. We corresponded for many years and swore that, when we both reached eighty, she would go to whatever the great square in Oslo was, and I would go to Trafalgar Square in London. I forget what we were supposed to do when we got to our respective squares, but I did remember to go.

There were a number of students from what was then Yugoslavia, which at that time was ruled by Marshal Tito, who was what they called a "strongman." Somehow, he kept the Serbians, Croatians, Bosnians, and the other ethnic groups together as one nation for a while. These students came with a "minder." He was a Communist Party member, and I think his job was to keep his eye on the youngsters and make sure they did not go astray. However, he liked to party, tell awful jokes, and chase the girls, so I don't think he created problems for any of his charges.

The two things I remember most about these students was one, their singing. They sang in beautiful harmonies the likes of which I had not heard before. The second thing was a strong drink they brought with them called *slivovitz*, a plum brandy that would knock out any inexperienced brandy drinker naive enough to try it.

It was at the Leverington camp that I first met Ken Murgatroyd, an ardent Manchester United supporter from Lancashire. Ken was an artist and became my lifelong friend. He was tall, with a David Niven-style mustache, and as easygoing as they come. I got to know many others at the camp whom I would stay in contact with for years as well.

There were four or five other NUS camps in the area around Leverington, all within a few miles of each other. They took turns in putting on the Friday night dances, and they would make great efforts to present the best-decorated "dance hall." There were many students studying for the Arts who came to the camps, and some of the presentations were spectacular. At the Leverington camp, they even painted the floor. For the ride to the neighboring camps for the dances, we piled into open lorries (trucks). There were very few safety regulations in the 1950s. Some of the facilities at the other camps were even more basic than at Leverington, but they were joyous places nonetheless.

When the weather was bad, which was quite often, we were sent to work in Smedleys Caning Factory in the nearby town of Wisbech. It was there that I had my strangest work experience ever. It was on the "pea belt." About six of us stood around a vibrating trampoline that stood at the bottom of a sloping, vibrating conveyor belt. This belt carried many hundreds of thousands, maybe many millions, of hot, steaming green peas. The bouncing peas appeared like a mighty horde of horsemen charging down the conveyor belt. When they reached the end, they tumbled onto the trampoline, and bounced their way across it before falling into a hopper.

It was the job of us pea watchers to look out for bad peas—bad in appearance, that is. When we saw one that did not look so good, we were to grab it in mid-bounce and throw it into a bucket. It is difficult to estimate the success rate of this operation, but it could not have been very high.

I went to Leverington for several seasons, but when Ken got a job as a cook in a NUS camp in Essex, I joined him. There we were to pick fruit for Wilkins and Sons, the company that makes the famous Tiptree jams that are known the world over. Tiptree Little Scarlet Strawberry jam was a favorite of James Bond.

The facilities at the Tiptree camp were far better than at Leverington—not luxurious, but for those days they were very good. There was a large, one-story brick building that had a very good and spacious kitchen at one end. The rest of the building served as a cafeteria, a place to relax, and on Friday nights it became a dance hall. For sleeping there was a permanent building for the women and tents for the men. There were good washing and toilet facilities, too. We lived quite well.

The students who came to Tiptree were even more international than at Leverington. More years had passed since the end of the war, and international travel and student exchanges were opening up—Yugoslavia, Scandinavia, Spain, the U.S.A., India, Italy, Nigeria, and on and on. As at Leverington, the students from abroad came to earn some money, to improve their English, and to get to know a different country. At the end of their stay, usually about four weeks, many would take the opportunity to go hitch-hiking, in those days a cheap and quite safe way to travel. Scotland was a favorite destination.

We worked in the fields during the day, picking strawberries, plums, apples, and all the other fruits that could be made into jam. Working alongside were the local village folk and "traveling people," most of whom came from Scotland. The local folks and the travelers were very experienced and fast pickers. They had worked at fruit picking since they were children. Also, the students from the East European countries were fast and hard workers. They had to be. Their governments allowed them to take only the equivalent of a few pounds with them when they traveled. They had to depend on what they earned to get by.

At the end of the work day, open lorries would take us back to the camp, where there was always a good dinner; after that was social time. There was plenty of talk. Some played chess, and some sang or listened to music. And as at Leverington, there were the dance nights. A Tiptree local named Chick, who had a radio and electrical store in the village, was the DJ. He had a large and good collection of records.

On a quieter note, there was a good local pub, the Ship. A popular place to hang out, it had a comfortable back room where the campers were welcomed by the landlord.

The fruit picking was the same routine as at Leverington, but the students were more integrated with other groups of pickers. Picking strawberries was hard. They grow on the ground, so you spend the day on one knee, and at the end of a long day it is hard to stand up straight. Each picker was assigned a long row of strawberries. Slow pickers, like me, would constantly look up to see if the end of the row was getting closer. A worker would start off with a basket in hand and five empty baskets tied around the waist with a piece of string. When a basket was filled it was left in the row and another basket was filled. When all six baskets were filled, they were carried back to the beginning of the row to be weighed. Each worker had a number, so the weight was recorded against the number, and that is how pay was determined. When you finished a row, you were assigned a new one.

There were two types of strawberries to be picked.

The first would go to the market, to be sold in the box that the picker had put them in. These were picked leaving the green leaves and the stalk on the strawberry. They were not washed, and I have always been careful since to wash fruit that is sold in the basket.

The second strawberry type were used for making jams; for these, the leaves and stalks had to be removed. This required a behavior called "thumbing"—pushing the thumb under the leaves to remove them.

Strawberry picking allowed for socialization. It was easy to talk to your neighbors in the adjacent rows. I was a slow picker, so my conversations did not last too long before my neighbor had pulled ahead. The local women could always be heard, however, some of them very loud and quite crude. They shouted across the rows and laughed as they described their husbands' proclivities in great detail. In my memory, the travelers kept themselves apart. A couple of farm laborers were always nearby to supervise the pickers. One of them was named Charlie. They were very friendly, and would remind us to "pick them all."

Picking apples was more fun, and while the strawberries started the season in June, the apples ended it in September, often the most wonderful month. In between we picked currants, berries, and plums, and on some days worked in the factory. For apples, you needed a ladder to pick the ones at the top of the tree. I remember once hearing an ear-piecing shriek in the apple orchard. A young German lad had slipped and slid down the rail of his ladder. He was taken to hospital with very swollen testicles.

The camp was managed by Abel, whom I had met at Leverington. Abel had been born in Germany, but when he was a boy, his family had fled to Rhodesia to escape the Nazis. He came to England as a young man and became involved with the National Union of Students. He had a lifelong love of classical music and played his collection of the great artists at all waking hours. He also loved to make announcements over the loudspeaker system. Whenever old campers get together, Abel's announcements are remembered.

In 1958, a lovely young student from Slovenia named Iva arrived at the camp. Abel noticed her and invited her to work in the kitchen. She was a big success, and eventually she and Abel married. The farmer built them a house on the campground, and there they lived and raised a son and a daughter.

The camp was, for Abel and Iva, their passion and their burden. When they retired, they moved to a big house in the ancient town of Colchester, taking with them some forty years of camp records, photographs, and memories. Abel died in 2012, but Iva is still in that house, and she remembers everyone and everything. Old campers from around the world still visit her, often bringing their children and now grandchildren. She welcomes them all with open arms and cups of hot tea. Iva has become more English than the English.

When my great friend Ken migrated from Leverington to join Abel, he came as a cook and worked in the kitchen with a wonderful fellow from Trinidad named Abraham and, later, with Iva. Other cooks and helpers were recruited from the campers—Briggita from Sweden, Dragitsa from somewhere in Yugoslavia, and a sparkling young woman from Croatia named Maria. She was an artist, and I liked her very much. Her English was limited, but she was very creative with the words she had. A beautiful Finnish girl took care of the little shop in the main hall. I think Ken and Abraham might have been a little naughty in the selection of young women to work in the kitchen. They always looked out for the new arrivals who came by lorry from Whitham Station on a Saturday afternoon. I found the Finns to be the most intriguing of all the nationalities.

Ken, still an avid Manchester United fan, had studied painting and had serious talent but did not realize his potential. To my knowledge, he only completed two paintings in oils—one, a fine self-portrait; and the other, a beautiful portrait, in profile, of his wife Metka, who, like Iva, was from Slovenia. I wish he had painted more. Before he married, Ken would take off for some place in Europe at the end of each season. He made many friends in the camp, and they all wanted him to visit them. I once joined Ken and two other Tiptree campers, Tony Ho and Terriki, a girl from Finland, in Paris.

Metka arrived at the camp speaking just a few words of English. She sang beautifully, and sometimes she and Iva sang songs from their native country in wonderful harmony. Ken got a permanent job with Wilkens, and he and Metka lived in a company house in the lovely village of Goldhanger, where they raised four children. Ken became seriously ill, and after a very hard and painful time for him and Metka, he died while still in his fifties. The Goldhanger church was packed to the rafters with friends and neighbors for his funeral service—a testament to how he was loved by all who knew him.

I remember very clearly two beautiful sisters who came from Malaga, in Spain: Maribel and Trini Cruz. They were happy, full of joy and laughter, and they enjoyed the camp life. Maribel wrote to me years later about her memories of the camp, and how she loved to hear Iva singing her beautiful Slovenian folk songs. Maribel had a doctorate in chemistry from Madrid University and spent her working life in research in Europe, and at the Universities of Purdue and Illinois in the U.S.A. At the end of her life, she was Mâitre de Recherche at the French National Centre for Scientific Research in France. An exalted position. I visited Maribel at Purdue University in the 1960s; she showed me around her department and introduced me to her workmates. We went to a garden party to meet her friends. I forget how long I was there, but before I left, I walked with her to the church where she attended Mass. She wore a mantilla on her head and looked very beautiful, and that was the last time I saw her. We corresponded for ten years, but Maribel wrote in Spanish, so I never really understood the full sense of her letters until many years later. She was forty-six when she died in France, in 1981, after a long illness. I learned of her sad death many years later by stumbling across her obituary in a magazine. Even after so many years, it was painful to read.

In these camps, with so many young folks from different cultures and backgrounds thrown together, there were romances, broken hearts, and vows made to keep in touch. Some were kept. I have forgotten many names but can still see the faces, and hear the laughter and the singing.

Returning to places you knew long ago, hoping to relive the past and re-unite with old friends, can be difficult. You are reminded that those days are gone forever, as are many of those you knew and loved. However, like the warrior's child, we can remember.

A CHANCE ENCOUNTER

I LEFT SCHOOL IN 1950 AT THE AGE OF FIFTEEN and immediately started looking for a job. Practically any line of work would do, as, in a little over two years, I would face the military draft when I turned eighteen. I was quite looking forward to the draft; my brother had spent his two years of National Service around Montego Bay in Jamaica, and his stories made it sound as if he'd had quite a good time. I looked through the "help wanted" advertisements in the newspaper and saw a couple of jobs that I could possibly do. They were both in Central London. I wrote a letter of application for one of the jobs and received a reply inviting me for an interview. I went for the interview and met with a small Dickensian figure named Mr. Laine. He was somewhere in his mid-sixties, and he told me that, if I took the job, I would be working for a Civil Engineering firm, and my job would mostly be running errands. I knew I could do that. The wages would be the magnificent sum of two pounds a week, and I would get two weeks' vacation every year. I took the job and found that the company specialized in piled foundation work.

The location was terrific, close to Covent Garden and the Drury Lane Theater. In good weather, I rode my bike to the office, but as there is a lot more bad weather than good, I generally took a tram car from Peckham to the Victoria Embankment and got off near to Waterloo Bridge; then I crossed the Strand and walked along the curve of The Aldwych, to Columbia House, where the company was located. I had to get up to the sixth floor, for this there was an ancient, manually operated, lift[1] controlled by a small, and grumpy, old man. He wore a cloth cap and had great difficulty making the floor of the clanking apparatus match the level of the landing. After several jolting attempts and being either nine inches too high or nine inches too low in all of them, he gave up, pulled the steel gates open, and said, "Mind the step." It was in this building that I began the twelve-year-long journey to becoming a professional engineer. I sometimes think, if only it had been the Old Vic that had needed an errand boy.

The work was easy—basically, I ran errands—but I did get some training on the drafting board and learned to draw engineering plans with an ink pen. I was given the opportunity to go to some construction sites to observe the pile-driving operations and was taught how to determine when a pile had been driven far enough into the ground to obtain its required bearing capacity. To do this, one used the Hiley Formula. One of the factors in the formula was called The Coefficient of Restitution, a fine phrase to throw around in any social gathering. Had it been a young girl who had got the job to run errands, she would not have been given these opportunities. At the time, despite the incredible work that women had done during the Second World War, technical work was still for men only.

People at the company were very interesting characters, and I listened to their stories. The older ones would have been born in the 1880s, some of them had fought in the trenches in the Great War, 1914–1918, and many of the younger men were veterans of the Second World War. These were men who had experienced cruel and hard times and had tales to tell. One described his exploits behind Japanese lines, and another his time as a rear gunner, or "Tail-End Charlie," in a Lancaster bomber. They were inspirational to a sixteen-year-old boy.

There were also some dubious characters. A small, roundly plump middle-aged man named Mr. Groyn was one of those. With rimless spectacles balanced on the end of a rather fat nose, he would express mock amazement by saying, "Well, I'll go to Heligoland in a bucket." Groyn was a flim-flam man. He knew how to sell the promise of easy money, and he managed to convince many of the higher-ups in the company that there was a fortune to be made by investing in his scheme to sell firewood. It was a Ponzi scheme, of course, and like all Ponzi schemes it eventually collapsed, and Groyn was fired. He probably made a profit, though, and he did make for some enjoyment among the junior staff, who got pleasure from seeing the bigwigs so easily taken to the cleaners.

The neighborhood around Columbia House was lively, and there was a great variety of things to do during lunch hour. I could go down to the Thames and watch the ships go by, or walk down Fleet Street, which in the 1950s was where the newspaper business was based. There were some good pubs in Fleet Street, but the legal drinking age was eighteen, and I had only just turned sixteen. I spent a lot of time in and around Covent Garden, near to the Opera House, where there were interesting shops and some cafes for a midday meal. When I didn't bring sandwiches from home, I usually ate in that area, but it was London in the 1950s, and the best I can say about the food is that it wasn't very good. There was one small but crowded cafe where I could get a two-course meal for one shilling and eleven pence. Once, when I ate there, I saw a large and very dead fly in my cabbage. When the bill came, I said to the waitress that I didn't think I should have to pay, as there was a dead fly in my lunch. She replied in a loud and strong Cockney voice that echoed throughout the cafe, "But it was only in *your* cabbage, wasn't it, luv." I had to admit that that was indeed the case. She then made a concession and said she would take three pence off of the bill.

I enjoyed the lunch time activities in Lincoln's Inn Fields, a large and beautiful public square that dates back to the 1600s. The wonderfully named Inigo Jones had had something to do with its layout. I have often thought that, if your surname is Jones, it is an advantage to have a name like Inigo to go with it.

Lincoln's Inn Fields was a beautiful and relaxing park, and a great place to eat one's sandwiches and buy a good cup of tea. During some months of the year, there were competitive netball games played by teams of women from companies in the central London area. They had a league and attracted good crowds. Netball looks a bit like basketball, but is a lot more genteel and the players are not allowed to run with the ball. When receiving the ball, a player has to stop and pass it from that spot. It was the same for shooting a basket. It was a game played by women and school girls all over Britain, rarely by men or boys. Maybe that has changed.

Now and again, a really big event absorbed the nation, one that caught the attention of all the people. One such event occurred in February 1952, when word came that King George VI had suddenly died in his big house in Norfolk. It was a bit of a shock—he was only fifty-seven years old at the time—but, we were told, he had not been well. There was much speculation about why he had died so suddenly. My aunt Lily was convinced that it was because he didn't keep his hat on in the cold weather. Aunt Lily knew a thing or two.

They brought the dead king back to London by train to Kings Cross Station, and there his coffin was placed on a horse-drawn gun carriage to be taken to Westminster Abbey, where he was to lie in state. To get to the Abbey, they had to bring him down the Grays Inn Road and pass close by the building where I worked. My boss, who was a very kind man, told me that I could take the rest of the day off to see King George go by, so I found a good viewing spot among the spectators who had already gathered.

As so often happens in London on great occasions, it rained. It was a really wet, unpleasant day, but, there was a large crowd—I suppose many bosses had given their workers time off to pay their last respects to the king. I had a good vantage point in the crowd and could look up Grays Inn Road and see the horses pulling the gun carriage, and the marching soldiers, as they proceeded towards me. There were no bands. The only sounds were the clip-clop of the horses' hooves and the clink of the harnesses, sounds that mingled with the footsteps of the soldiers escorting the coffin. The crowd, wrapped in raincoats, was silent. Men took off their hats and held them to their hearts as King George passed by, and many in the crowd wept for him. They remembered that, against the urging of his ministers, he had refused to leave London during the wartime blitz, and so Londoners had a warm spot in their hearts for him. When the gun carriage passed where I stood, I was overwhelmed by the solemnity of it all. I had a good view of the mourners. Among them was that bounder the Duke of Windsor, the older brother of the late king. He was in exile at the time and had flown to London for the funeral. It was the only time I ever saw him, but that was no loss; he didn't seem to have been of much use to anyone.

When the procession had passed, I didn't have to go back to work; I had the rest of the day to myself. It is likely that I wandered into Lincoln's Inn Fields to listen to the soapbox orators. There were always at least two of them at opposite corners of the park, ranting away on their pet subjects. They came in all shapes and sizes, and some of them were quite brilliant. There were many public-speaking venues in London, Speakers Corner in Hyde Park being the most famous, but I liked Lincoln's Inn the best. The speakers held forth on every subject under the sun—religion, reincarnation, Socialism as opposed to Communism, and so on. The Communist speaker was very amusing and did a great impression of Winston Churchill. The speakers had to contend with hecklers, of course, but they were rarely bested by the interrupters.

One of the most popular speakers in the Fields was an interesting fellow named Tony Turner. Small in stature, he was a leading light in the Socialist Party of Great Britain, an organization with a long history but not many members. They were believers in Marxism, though through the ballot box, not armed revolution, and they did not seem to like the Soviet Union, calling them state capitalists. They believed in something called "the theory of impossibilism"; I had no idea what that meant, which could explain why they did not get many votes. Tony Turner was their most lucid advocate, but he and the party had a falling out over something or other and went their own ways. Tony was born in New Zealand, but his mother, who was London Irish, had brought him to a tough part of South

London when he was an infant. He'd been raised in the Elephant and Castle district. You can't get more London than that.

The SPGB never had many members, but they had many skillful debaters, and they took on all comers. By presenting their case in a vigorous manner, they did wield some influence. A lot of that was due to Tony Turner, who was well known to be a mighty speaker. The Thunderous Voice of Socialism, he was called. One of Tony's stock lines was directed to the working man and woman. "You go to work to earn the money, to buy the food, to get the energy, to go to work, to earn the money. . . ." His ideas were somewhat extreme. He believed in a return to a pre-industrial means of production which did not seem like the best approach to getting elected.

Ten years or so later, in the early 1960s, I was living and working in East Africa and spent some time in the beautiful and fascinating city of Nairobi, Kenya. A popular gathering place in the city was the Thorn Tree Sidewalk Cafe in what was then the New Stanley Hotel.[2] Founded in 1882, it was the oldest hotel in the city. I was sitting by myself at a small table, enjoying a pot of tea and observing the comings and goings of people, when a spanking new Mercedes Benz drove up, an expensive but popular car in East Africa among those who could afford it, as it was very strong on the rough dirt roads. There were only about three hundred miles of paved roads in the territory at that time. The door of the Mercedes opened, and a small, tanned man got out, looking to be somewhere in his fifties. He strode into the café, sat down at the table next to mine, and ordered a drink. I felt there was something familiar about him and was sure that I had seen him before—not in Africa, but somewhere else, maybe back in England. I wracked my brains to put a name to the face. Then it just hit me: Tony Turner. I was so confident it was he that I leaned over and said, "Excuse me, but are you Tony Turner"?

He seemed delighted to be recognized, and said that indeed he was.

We started up a conversation, and I told him I remembered him as an orator in Lincoln's Inn Fields in London. At that, he got up and joined me at my table. We ordered some drinks and talked about his time as a political leader of the SPGB, and of London in the 1950s. He said he'd had to resign from the party over a disagreement on the "nature of socialism." He also told me something about his life: He had been in the Royal Navy and worked at a number of "survival" jobs; he also had had a large family, I forget how many children, but the number was way above the norm. He had also been a successful amateur boxer and the chess champion of Kenya. Tony had tried his hand at many things and had been prepared to take risks.

After a while, I knew I had to ask him the burning question. How did it come about that he, a fundamental socialist who believed that no person should have more than his neighbor, was driving around East Africa in a Mercedes Benz. He then told me that he had permanently moved to Kenya, which he liked a lot, and had done quite well in selling encyclopedias. He'd later expanded and opened up a very successful book-selling business in Kenya, which had made him a lot of money. He was thriving. Tony, like most folks, had found that being able to afford some of life's luxuries was very pleasant.

Tony died in Cape Town, South Africa, in 1992. A committed socialist who became a successful capitalist, he had led an interesting and colorful life. I am glad that I bumped into him in that sidewalk café; it was a most amazing chance encounter.

Chance encounters can be gifts to remember, or they can be awkward and uncomfortable. This encounter with Tony Turner brought back good memories of London in the 1950s, my first job, lunch hours in Lincoln's Inn Fields, and King George. So it wasn't so bad. Tony was a brilliant and entertaining man, although some of his political ideas did seem to me to be a bit far out. However, as the saying goes, "It takes all sorts."

Endnotes

1. What is called a "lift" in England is referred to as an "elevator" in the United States.

2. The New Stanley Hotel has since been renamed the Sarova Stanley. It was originally named for the Welsh explorer Sir Henry Morton Stanley, who gained fame for being the guy who, in 1871, found the missionary and explorer David Livingstone in the jungle, somewhere near Lake Tanganyika. It is likely that Livingstone didn't even know that he was lost. Stanley's immortal words on meeting Livingstone, were: "Doctor Livingstone, I presume?"

THE MOUNTAIN AND THE SERGEANT

Climbing Mount Kilimanjaro

IN THE SUMMER OF 1960, I WAS WORKING as a structural engineer in the City of London, very near St. Brides Church on Fleet Street. The church, a Christopher Wren masterpiece, had a pleasant and peaceful churchyard where, when the weather permitted, I would take my lunch and read the newspaper. One lunch time, looking in the jobs column in the *Daily Telegraph*, I saw that a structural engineer was wanted in Dar es Salaam, the capital of what was then Tanganyika.

I did some research on Tanganyika and found that, until the First World War, it had been a German colony. After that war, the League of Nations, I think it was, took control of the country, and then handed it over to Britain—lock, stock, and barrel. No one, it seems, had bothered to ask the indigenous people of Tanganyika what they thought about that, but so it was in colonial times. So Tanganyika became, along with Uganda and Kenya, a part of British East Africa.

Some geography books, and a movie, *The African Queen*, sold me on the attraction of living and working in East Africa. So I applied for, and got, the job.

I set about learning what I could about East Africa and what I would need to live there. There was a lot to learn. What special items should I take with me? An article I read said I would have to bring lots of salt pills, as the heat would drain the salt out of my blood. I didn't like the sound of that, so I got lots of salt pills. I went to a tropical clothing outfitter in Bond Street and bought a bunch of snazzy lightweight suits and other items the salesman said I would need. Later I learned that New York City could be just as hot, and that the general workday outfit for European men in East Africa was shorts, a shirt, shoes, and socks. The socks should come up to just below the knees, of course.

In September 1960 I was on my way to Dar es Salaam. I flew out from London in a British Airways prop plane that made three stops on the way. We changed planes in Nairobi and finally got to Dar. On disembarking and crossing the tarmac, I was struck by the air of Africa—it was sweet and scented. It was more than exciting, it was exhilarating.

I was met by Jeff Taylor, who ran the small consulting firm I was joining. Jeff was a burly Yorkshireman who was always threatening to thump someone in the ear. He was known as "Thump 'Em in the Ear Taylor." He took me to the New Africa Hotel, where I would be staying until I found permanent quarters. A fine old building close to the harbor, it had been built by the Germans around 1900. With walls three feet thick and a slow- moving ceiling fan, the rooms in the hotel were surprisingly cool.

I had brought my guitar with me from England, and after I had unpacked my suitcase, I thought I would relax for awhile by playing some of tunes I had learned at the Spanish Guitar Center in London. I opened the case and was shocked to see what looked more like a boomerang than a guitar. No one had told me that you must loosen the strings on any stringed instrument before taking it onto an airplane. My guitar was destroyed—an unfortunate beginning to my African sojourn.

After a few weeks, I moved into a nice apartment, and it seemed that all was going well. Then I found that a house servant came with the apartment. He was a pleasant young Tanganyikan fellow named Hector. The problem for me was, I did not need or want a servant. I could fix my own breakfast and wash my own clothes. Apart from that, the idea of having a servant was an embarrassment. I would certainly get laughed at by my mates back in South East London.

The problem for Hector, and, as it turned out, for me, was that this was his job, and he was supporting a family on his earnings. He sent money home to his village. I just could not bring myself to tell Hector that I did not need his services, so I kept paying him, even though there was very little for him to do. On the upside, I did practice speaking Swahili with him, but, in the evening, I had to drive him home. So it turned out that I became Hector's chauffeur.

I soon settled in and started to explore Dar. It sits on the east coast of Africa, smack on the equator, and has a graceful natural harbor that provides open access to the Indian Ocean. The exotic island of Zanzibar lies about forty miles off the coast. Dar is the capital of Tanganyika, which was, along with its neighbors Kenya and Uganda, gearing up for independence from Britain. This would come to pass for all three countries within the next three years, but in 1960 there were still British governors who would have looked at home in a Gilbert and Sullivan operetta. They wore white suits and large, rather comical, white hats bedecked with enormous feathers.

Dar was a very cosmopolitan town. and the population of around 200,000 was a lively mix of people, cultures, and religions. The majority were indigenous Africans from various parts of Tanganyika. There were many folks whose ancestral home was the subcontinent of India. Their grandparents had come to East Africa to work on building the railroads, chosen to stay, and flourished. An interesting group came from Goa, a Portuguese enclave on the west coast of India. These were very handsome people, and very Catholic. The Greeks owned the sisal plantations and were involved in the rope trade. They were successful and quite well to do. Finally, there were the people who thought they were running the show, the British in their long shorts. I was one of them. Sadly, these different groups were not socially well connected.

I enjoyed life in Dar, but it was hot, and air conditioners were a rarity. I can't remember riding in a car or a bus, or working in a building, that had air conditioning. Then I was introduced to the African American Institute (AAI) by an American friend who worked there named Ronald. It was a haven, and a gold mine for so many things—books, magazines, and records, even records of Pete Seeger, which were hard to come by in the U.S.A. in those days. He was on some sort of government blacklist for being a bit more progressive in his thinking than some folks in the American government liked.

There were many reasons to go to the AAI—it was a popular place, and it was the first time in my life I had been in an air-conditioned building. It was a great relief in the full heat of the day. A popular bar drew customers to hear a very good Goan jazz band. I went there with an African American named Dave Oswald, who had been a jazz critic back in the U.S. Dave said he was in East Africa to study German/East African history, although no one ever saw him studying anything. He was a great fellow. When Louis Armstrong and his band came to town, Dave introduced me to his friend Trummy Young, the trombonist for the great man; we took him to the town market to see some colorful local life. Dave and I enjoyed joining Ron and his wife, Jacqueline, for dinner at their house in the woods. Jacqueline was a magical cook and the most delightful hostess.

Some English colonial types had taken it upon themselves to show Louis and his band members around the town. They thought that these Americans would be impressed by a ten-story apartment building that had recently been built in Dar. It is tough to impress folks from Chicago and New York City with a ten-story building. I did once, however, find myself sitting one empty bar stool away from Louis Armstrong at the New Africa Hotel bar. How can you beat that? Louis was joined by his wife, and they were both dressed "to the nines," for dinner.

Other delights of Dar were tea rooms that could have been plucked straight out of villages in Gloucestershire, and funky, slightly sleazy bars where old-timers gathered, including a well-known local smuggler named Kloser. Once, as I sat in one of these bars, a gigantic cockroach fell from the ceiling and landed in my beer with a splash. Those cockroaches were as big as a blacksmith's thumb. Saturday mornings were fun, with a gathering of beer drinkers at the Tusker Brewery, followed by an excellent curry lunch at the New Africa Hotel—a great way to start the weekend.

Different ethnic groups had their own clubs and sports teams.

The Gymkhana Club was where British folks went. They played cricket and football against Goan, Indian, and African clubs. The games were well played, intense, and, it must be said, quite friendly. It was too bad, however, that the social mores of the time and place prevented the teams from socializing *after* a game. I wish that we could have gathered together at the bar and gotten to know each other and, hopefully, have a good time.

I liked to sit outside the New Africa Hotel in the late evening with Dave Oswald, when the bar was officially closed. The night watchman would fry up some fish for Dave and me that he had caught that day, and sing us some songs in his own language. Many of the indigenous African people were fluent in three languages— Swahili, English, and their own tribal tongue. This gave pause to those of us who had struggled for years to learn some French but still had a hard time putting together a sentence.

For my job, I traveled to many parts of East Africa, and fascinating travel it was. In Karamoja in northern Uganda, where life was still much the way it had been in the nineteenth century, the men went totally naked while the women were fully clothed. I worked on a number of interesting projects, including the design of a church in Mwanza, at the southern end of Lake Victoria. I never got to see the church completed, but hopefully it still stands. In Kampala, my favorite East African town, I worked for a small consulting firm named Roughton, Campbell, and Fitzgerald. I visited the Serengeti Game Park, and the white sands of Mombasa. I once flew a small plane over Lake Rudolph in Northern Kenya, to see the flamingos. I circled it low around the mouth of a volcano. I hasten to say that I did not take the plane off the ground or land it; my flight companion, who was the pilot, did that. While in the air, I took the controls so he could take some photographs.

Because there were only three hundred miles of paved road in the three East African countries, car journeys were long, bumpy, tiring, and very dusty. When driving to a distant job site, I would often pick up a traveler— a schoolteacher walking to the school in the next village, or a mother, with a baby on her back, walking many miles to the clinic. The local people had to walk to get anywhere; they had no cars, and buses were rare. Their patience in taking these long, necessary walks was remarkable.

Travel on dirt roads had its problems. Here I came around the bend a little too fast. I got out unscathed and waited for help. A bus filled with young men on their way to a football game came along. They were a good-humored bunch; they flipped my car upright and went on their way.

During journeys into the back country far away from any town, one could often find a cozy, old-world inn built by the British settlers of long ago. Who would expect such a taste of Olde England in a land where elephants, giraffe, and zebra roamed? The inns were set in quiet spots and were surrounded by English gardens. Traditional

British fare was served. Meat pies, plum puddings with custard, and tea were brought to your room at 6:00 a.m. whether you wanted it or not. It was impossible not to get your pot of tea at 6:00 a.m. English people drink tea at 6:00 a.m., and that was that.

The die-hard British colonists did not socialize with the African and Indian populations. They criticized, and shunned, those who liked to play football and cricket against local teams or enjoyed the great bands from the Congo when they played at the local beer halls. They could not accept the notion that independence for the peoples of the East African countries was on its way, and that their days of being in charge would soon be over.

After about a year of work, during which time I learned some rudimentary Swahili, I had earned some vacation time. Many ex-patriates would travel back to Britain for vacations, some to visit their children, whom they kept locked away in boarding schools. They called it "going home on leave." I chose to stay in East Africa and do something adventurous. I decided I would climb the highest mountain in Africa and the highest free- standing mountain in the world, Mount Kilimanjaro. I had met an English fellow named Bill Ford who also wanted to climb it, so we teamed up to make the three-hundred-mile journey over the rough, dusty dirt roads from Dar to a lovely town called Moshi, which sits in the foothills of the great mountain. There we would find a place to stay for the night, look for a guide, and get some boots and climbing gear.

We saw some incredible sights on the journey—wildlife, spec-tacular landscapes, and interesting people. At one point, we were flagged down by the driver of a large truck that had broken down, and the driver, a white guy, was waiting for help, which, he said, was on the way. He asked for some water, which we gave him, along with some food, to help him through his wait. The remarkable thing was, the driver had only one arm. Driving those roads in East Africa is tough enough with two arms; how he managed, I don't know.

A constant sight was the fat-bottomed baobab trees, sometimes called the African upside-down tree. The trunks are fat and the branches look like roots. The story of these trees is that God got fed up with having them in Paradise, so he threw them over the wall and they landed upside down in East Africa. Not a bad story.

Eventually, we pulled in to Moshi and could really see the mountain. Kilimanjaro, at 19,341 feet high, is sometimes called the roof of Africa. It was covered at the top with glistening ice and snow, and a ring of cloud hung just below the peak, like a smoke ring. "Moshi" is the Swahili word for "smoke." The mountain has three extinct, or dormant, volcanic cones—Mawenzi, Shira, and Kibo; this last is the highest peak, and the one we were headed for. It was a stunning sight, especially when seen from afar. We took a couple of rooms in a local inn and asked for advice on hiring a guide and where to get climbing gear. Well, they said, they could help us right there. They would provide a guide and the gear we needed for the climb. I should have paid more attention during the outfitting, as the boots they gave me turned out to be much too big. I was to pay for this mistake on the way down from the mountain top.

Being outfitted at the same time was a young German woman named Inga. She was set to make the climb, so we decided to join forces and venture together. The next day, we were introduced to our guide, a very pleasant older man. I forget which tribe he was from, probably Chagga, a local people known to be very good farmers. He had been born and raised around the mountain, and he brought with him some porters, as, in addition to warm clothing and provisions, we had to carry our own firewood up the mountain.

On the evening before the start of our great adventure, Bill, Inga, and I sat on the veranda of the inn, drinking local beer and gazing at the mountain peak. It looked impossible for us, three totally inexperienced climbers. Did we really think we could climb all the way to the top? I guess we did. We all retired to bed and were awakened at 6:00 a.m. by the inevitable pot of tea being brought to our rooms. We had breakfast and prepared for the day.

Mount Kilimanjaro does not present many climbing challenges. There are a couple of places where one has to scramble, but there is no need for driving spikes into the mountain face or hanging from ropes. It is basically a long, slow, hard slog. The problem is the altitude, and that is a big problem. Rushing straight for the upper slopes before getting acclimatized can lead to acute mountain sickness.

Climbing party in the grass on the lower slopes.
Inga is on the right, the guide front center

We left Moshi early in the morning for the starting point of the climb, where we met our guide. He took us at an easy walking pace along the trail, which soon brought us into misty rain forests. It was exciting, and the scenery was breathtaking. We were on our way!

When evening came we stopped at the Mandara hut, the first of the exotically named huts that we would use for sleeping. The others were the Horombo hut and then the Kibo huts, which were on the saddle of the mountain at about 15,500 feet, directly below the peak. In those days, the huts were nothing more than rudimentary shelters with no services at all.

We were in good shape until around 14,000 feet. After that, breathing became difficult; we got severe headaches, and walking became a slow stop-and-start effort. Our hearts were racing at many times the normal rate.

As we got higher, the plant life turned from lush vegetation to scrubby, tough, short growth, and it got colder. It took three days and nights to reach the saddle, where we walked on rough and stony ground, and it was very cold. We walked slowly, "pole pole" as they say in Swahili, stopping every thirty paces or so to allow our heartbeats to slow down. In the far distance we could see the Kibo huts at the foot of the steep slopes that would take us to the top of the mountain. The plan was to stay in the huts for the first part of the night and then, in the wee small hours, get up, have some breakfast, and start the final ascent before the first daylight.

It was a long, slow, and exhausting walk, and the huts didn't seem to be getting closer. Inga was strong and would pull ahead of Bill and me; I thought that if any one of us made it to the top, it would be her.

Eventually, we got to those huts. It was cold, so we lit a fire,

*The mountain, with Kibo huts in the distance. At about
16,000 feet, walking is slow and hard.*

cooked a meal, and then prepared for a short sleep. All was going
according plan when—from out of the blue—a party made up of
British army officers, a very loud British sergeant, and a bunch of
African army cadets appeared on the scene with four horses. It was
a big surprise to us. They had climbed up from the other side of the
mountain and were on a training mission for the cadets.

The one giving the orders was the sergeant, a character straight
out of central casting. He was very loud. After brief introductions
and a bit of a chat, one of the officers asked if they could join us
and use the services of our guide. I said they could, but after it was
all over, I thought I had been a bit high-handed in saying so without
consulting the guide. I hope they paid him something, but I doubt
that they did.

We all went to bed, still clothed in our climbing outfits, and tried
to sleep. In the very small hours of the morning, we were awakened

Horses used by the army party to carry equipment up the mountain

by our guide, who said it was time to get up and get ready to go. It was still dark, and was very cold when we crawled out of our sleeping bags. Someone had boiled up the coffee and prepared a rudimentary breakfast. I forget what the breakfast consisted of, but we ate it, then got set to go. Inga, our German friend, who had been so strong until that point, said she would not continue. I tried to get her to change her mind, but she would not. Maybe she was upset by the additional company, or of being the only woman in a group of twenty or so men, I don't know. I am sure she would have made it to the top. So we started off without her. I learned later that, when daylight came, she made her way down the slopes, back to Moshi. We never saw her again. She must have been bitterly disappointed, and I was sorry for her. Bill Ford was still with us, if not as enthusiastic as he had been a few days before, but he was ready to give it a shot.

The first target was Gilmans Point, on the rim of the crater, about six hundred feet below the highest peak of the mountain, which was then called "Kaiser Wilhelm Spitze" after the German emperor. After independence in 1961 the name was changed to "Uhuru," or "Freedom," Peak. Most climbers call it a day at Gilmans Point, as it is about a two-hour trek around the crater to Uhuru, and two hours back—a long way for not much extra in altitude and the day quickly fading. The footing for the climb from the Kibo Huts to Gilmans was difficult—a mixture of loose stones, snow, and ice, called "scree." You would take a step forward and then your foot would slip back a half step as the stones moved.

We rested in a cave at about two thousand feet from the top, then started again. It was still dark. Bill Ford had developed terrible stomach cramps and was bent over double; it was clear that he was in trouble. He said he could not go on, so we had to leave him to make his way down the mountain. I was in very bad shape and short of breath, my head pounding, and I had painful cramps. I had a hard job forcing one foot in front of the other and was about to quit. At that point, one of the young African cadets collapsed on the mountain side. He was groaning and in great distress. His comrades went to help him, but the loud and awful sergeant shouted, "Leave him! He's got no guts." Well, now I could not quit—I had to go on. We left the poor cadet to get himself together and make his way down to the Kibo huts, and we started off again. Our guide would go on ahead of us, then stop, sit on a rock, and watch us climb towards him. He had a little flute on which he played tunes. He was mocking us. Spending so much of his life on the mountain, he was not bothered by the altitude.

As the first gray light of dawn broke through, I was getting a second wind. I pushed ahead of everyone but the guide. We were almost at Gilmans Point and the sergeant was coming up on my shoulder. He really wanted to be first to the Point, but I was not going to let him pass. I forced myself ahead, leaving him behind, until I found myself standing alone on the roof of Africa. It was a good place for photos; after taking some scenic shots, I handed my camera to the sergeant and asked him to take my picture. I struck a suitably mountaineering pose, and he got down on one knee, fiddled with the focus quite a bit, then took the shot.

At Gilmans Point—but no legs, no mountain, and a pants problem. Was it the sargeant's revenge?

It was a beautiful morning, the cloud cover gone, and the sky was a startling blue. I looked down the mountain, first at the incredible view stretching for miles before and beneath me, and then at the stragglers fighting their way up. Maybe forty percent of the original party made it to Gilmans Point. The army party had decided that this was as near to the top as they wanted to go, so after a rest, they began to head back to the Kibo huts. That left just me and the guide. He was still full of energy. We took off on the long walk around the blue-iced rim of the crater to Uhuru Peak. I can't recall if, at that time, there was any marker for the highest point, but I took the guide's word for it that I was at the top. I could have been a few feet short. I was standing on top of the highest freestanding mountain in the world, and it was glorious.

I spent some time taking in the view, but I was not feeling well. The brief flow of adrenalin I had felt in the dash to be the first to stand on Gilmans Point had gone. The altitude and thin air were now taking a toll, and it was time to start back down the stony, snow covered-slope, back to the Kibo huts some four thousand feet below. We made our way back to Gilmans Point and then to the huts.

The wise thing to do is to take your time when going down from a high altitude, and let your body adjust. But it was too easy to almost run and slide down the stony scree, and I went too fast. The sudden change in air pressure gave me an intense and very painful headache. It felt as though my skull was opening and shutting. I sat down for awhile to adjust, then started, with some others, to walk down the mountain. My feet were by then very painful. The oversized boots had caused mammoth blisters. I think we may have stopped overnight at the Mandara hut, but whether we did or not, we eventually got back to the Inn in Moshi. I finally took my boots off and looked at the bloody mess that was my feet. The blisters were the size of chicken's eggs. I was told of an old retired German doctor who could help me. I found him. He looked exactly like the German actor Eric Von Stroheim, and he had been living by the mountain since the First World War. He popped the egg-sized blisters on my feet and fixed me up with some bandages. I gave him ten shillings and went on my way.

I found Bill Ford, and together we drove back to Dar es Salaam, a rough and dusty journey, but I was very content. In Dar I had the photos developed. There were a couple of good shots of Bill Ford and Inga, and of the ascent, and some very good ones of the mountain. I did like the photo of the horses at 15,500 feet, and the picture I took of the sergeant standing on the Point was quite good. Then there was the picture that he took of me at Gilmans Point—what a disaster. It showed me from the waist up with a clear blue sky for a background and a serious pants problem. There was nothing to show that I was actually standing on top of Mount Kilimanjaro. In fact, there was no mountain at all. The sergeant had had the last laugh.

With no photographic evidence that I had actually stood on top of the mountain, you might not believe that I had, but there was a book in a box somewhere up there in which all climbers who reached the summit signed their names, as did I. It may still be there, so if you don't believe my story, you can climb up the mountain and search for that book. You will be sure to see my name.

I am glad that we did meet those soldiers and cadets by the Kibo Huts; otherwise, there would not be much of a story. I do also wish that the British army sergeant had been more careful when taking my photograph and included the mountain under my feet. But sometimes I wonder whether it really was his revenge for me not letting him get to the top first.

TODAY, CLIMBING THE MOUNTAIN has become a big part of the East African tourist industry. At any given time, there are thousands of climbers scrambling to the top, lining up to stand at the peak to have their picture taken, and, sadly, leaving trash scattered over the climbing trails. I don't think I would want to climb that mountain today with so many other people, but if I did, I would be sure to get better-fitting boots. In 1961, until we met the sergeant and the army party, we had it all to ourselves—that glorious mountain, and just our small group, slowly making our way up to the "Roof of Africa."

NOTES ON LIFE
IN UGANDA

I DID NOT STAY LONG IN DAR ES SALAAM after my return from Mount Kilimanjaro. I had found work with an engineering consultancy named Roughton, Campbell and Fitzgerald, in Kampala, the capital of Uganda, and was planning a move. I did stay long enough, however, to see Tanganyika gain its independence from Britain, the first of the three East African countries to do so. There were great celebrations. and it was a hoot to see the white-suited British governor, wearing his big white hat, hand over the keys of the government to the local lads, led by Julius Nyerere who would become the President.

I took the opportunity to go to some sessions of the new parliament and found it quite bewildering. It was based entirely on the Westminster model, complete with the ceremonial figure of Black Rod, in satin knee britches no less. What Black Rod could have in common with the culture and history of East Africa, I don't know. It is a position that dates back to fourteenth-century England, and one of Rod's duties is to serve as the doorkeeper at meetings of the Most Noble Order of the Garter. I don't think it took long for the folks in Tanganyika to realize that there was not much Black Rod could do for them.

Soon after this, I packed my belongings and drove my Citroen ID19 the one thousand miles of dusty roads to Kampala. It took a couple of days, and when I arrived, I cleaned up a bit, then took a walk around the center of the town. Kampala was hot but not unbearably so, and everyone dressed for the weather. The most prominent sight was the brand-new parliament building, and there was a lively downtown where I found a place to eat. I then made my way to the office where I would be working and met the man who would be my boss. He was a balding and bearded Dane of medium height named Ib Hansen. He was very impressive and friendly, and soon put me at my ease as he showed me where my work station would be and described what sort of work was current in the office.

Until I could find permanent accommodation, Ib had arranged temporary lodging for me in a large rooming house not far from the center of town. They were comfortable lodgings; all tenants had a good-sized room, and the bathrooms were shared, as was a large balcony where residents could gather in the evenings. I soon realized, however, that many secret assignations and licentious activities took place behind the walls of the establishment. The rooming house had a reputation.

The lodgers were an interesting lot, and one in particular was *very* interesting. He was a crew-cut American named John Thalmayer, and he was a union organizer. In the U.S.A., he had been a member of the International Brotherhood of Teamsters, working alongside Jimmy Hoffa. John was a tough guy, about forty years old and powerfully built, and he was in Uganda working for the International Federation of Building Workers. His challenge was to organize the building workers in Uganda into a union. This, as he found out, was no easy task. Unions were a new concept in East Africa at that time, and John had a hard time keeping the various union "locals" in business.

What I remember most about him is that he had a mine of stories and was a fine singer. Most of his stories, which he told so well, were of union struggles and his role in them. Along with his stories, he sang songs of labor in a strong bass baritone voice. He was also very good company and taught me a number of those songs; "Which Side Are You On" was one.

The work that came into the consultancy was good and plentiful, and gave me many opportunities to travel throughout Uganda. I drove all over the country, from the dry and very poor region of Karamoja in the northeast, to Mwanza, sitting at the southern end of Lake Victoria. Several times I drove close to the Uganda–Congo border, which at that time was in great turmoil.

Independence had come to what had been the Belgian Congo in 1960, and soon after, with, it is said, some scurrilous help from the CIA, the democratically elected president, Patrice Lumumba, was assassinated. For the next five years, the country was torn by warring factions and plunged into anarchy. It was not looking good for the Belgian settlers, who had been living very well since the reign of King Leopold II, who, in the 1880s, had made the Congo his personal property. Leopold, who went on to amass a huge fortune from the ivory and rubber trades, was responsible for the deaths of millions of the indigenous people. It is no wonder, then, that when independence came, the Belgian settlers thought it time to get out, and get out they did. The flight peaked around 1963, and it was a pitiful sight to see them as they fled with their families across the border into Uganda. They left everything they could not stuff into a car behind them. What became of them all, I don't know.

Much of Uganda is made up of The Kingdom of Buganda, which included Kampala. The Kingdom dates back to the twelfth century and had, until well into the twentieth, a ruler who was known as the Kabaka. At one time the Kabaka was all-powerful, but his political position was now in decline. I never saw him but did see his palace and the many beautiful peacocks that lived there. The Prime Minister of Uganda was a very corrupt guy named Milton Obote. He found the Kabaka to be a nuisance and ordered one of his enforcers to take some soldiers to get rid of him.

The enforcer was none other than the notorious Idi Amin. It did not take long—the Kabaka's forces were no match for Big Idi and his gang. The Kabaka did escape, however, and went into exile in England, where, within a few years, he died in the East End of London. Obote abolished the Kingdom of Buganda in 1964. (It was reinstated in 1993.) He got his comeuppance when Amin decided he wanted to run the show himself and so forced Milton into exile. Some years later, Obote made a comeback, and then Amin was out. Between them, these two just about destroyed the beautiful country, and the people, of Uganda, but they both lived into their eighties and were kept in great comfort while in exile. So much for justice.

Much of my engineering work was related to designing new storage facilities for the coffee trade, a staple of the Ugandan economy.

I made the first surveys of a construction site where a complex of storage buildings was to be built, and ran into a problem. My survey line was interrupted by a primitive outhouse. I had to negotiate with the outhouse owner, and come up with some form of compensation to encourage him to relocate it. After some back and forth, we came to a financial agreement, and he relocated his outhouse. The design of the complex was complicated by it being on sloping ground, but a political decision had been made, and that was where it had to be built.

I left Uganda before the complex was completed, but in 1967, while in Canada, I went to the Montreal World Fair and found the Uganda Pavilion. I went in and encountered a splash of nostalgia—there were so many things I recognized and remembered. Among the exhibits, I found an enormous colored photograph. It was of the completed coffee storage complex, with an explanatory write-up discussing the importance of the coffee trade to the economy of Uganda. I stood by the photograph for a long time, hoping someone would ask me a question, but no one did.

I made many friends in Kampala, among them two guys in the newspaper business. One was an American named Keith, the other an English fellow named Johnny South. What a great name for a newspaper reporter! Johnny wrote for the *Uganda Argus*, while Keith sent reports on East Africa to an American newspaper. There were many others whose names I have forgotten, but I do remember the long weekend trips we made to the white sands of Mombasa.

Mombasa was a fascinating and wonderful town, heavy with exotic Arabic influences. We primarily went there for the glorious beaches and to swim in the Indian Ocean, but during one visit, and in one of life's amazing chance encounters, I bumped into an old friend. His name was Tony Berry, and we had both been members of the same running club in South East London, the Deptford Park Harriers. To recover from a broken romance, Tony had set out to travel the world but had paused in Mombasa, where he had found work at a beach hotel. The last I heard of him was a letter he wrote to me from Australia, where he had later settled.

Along with Keith and Johnny South, I enjoyed going to an African nightspot called Top Life. Great bands from the Congo played there, and they always brought in a good crowd. It was amazing whom you would see at Top Life, once I spotted the chief of the Uganda police, a white guy, having a great time. However, as in Tanganyika, the British "way to behave" folks frowned on social-izing with non-white people, and we were berated by these very bor-ing folk for "letting the side down."

I have always had a passion for track and field, and in the 1960s I was writing a column on the East African athletics scene for an English magazine. I had seen astonishing potential from the runners and jumpers in the rest of East Africa and wanted to find out what was happening in Uganda. I had a reference to contact an English guy named Paddy Field. Yes, that was his name. He was an officer in the Ugandan police force and a very good runner. He held the Ugandan police force record for the mile, with a time of four minutes and twenty-five seconds—a *very* good time considering the condi-tions of the running tracks. To introduce myself, I called him on the phone, and he invited me to come down to the Police Training School grounds to see the athletes in training. I went to the grounds on the outskirts of Kampala, where the track and field athletes were sharing the facilities with the boxers. I watched the Ugandan run-ners train, and their quality and potential were immediately appar-ent.

One Ugandan runner was particularly interesting—Deogatius Rabugwene, a very good distance runner and an amusing storyteller.

He was selected to run the marathon for Uganda, in the 1962 Empire Games (later called the Commonwealth Games) in Australia. The top marathoner at that time was an Englishman named Brian Kilby, who was going to run in the same race. When the race was underway, Kilby soon went into the lead and Deogatius, our young hero decided to go with him. They ran together for many miles, and Kilby must have been wondered who this little guy was—but Deogatius had a problem. His shorts were much too big, and he had to keep pulling them up. He later related, in a very entertaining way, his story of the race, in which he finished eleventh, referring to Kilby as "that terrible Mzungu" (a Swahili word that basically means "white guy"). Terrible or not, Kilby easily won the race.

I became an official in the Ugandan Amateur Athletic Association and officiated at a number of track and field meetings, usually as a timekeeper. It was at one of these meetings that I first saw the great Kenyan champion Kipchoge Keino run. At that time, he was unknown outside of East Africa, but in a few years, that would change. He went on to become a double Olympic Champion, and a track immortal. In the 1968 Mexico City games he won a gold medal in the 1500-Meters, and in the 1972 Munich games, he took home the gold for the Steeplechase. He led the way for East African athletes to revolutionize and dominate the world of middle- and long-distance running.

In addition to my involvement in track and field, I joined a mostly British football team. We had some good games with other local teams and, on one memorable occasion, played a team of prisoners in a local jail. The prisoners were tightly packed around the touch lines, and to take a throw in, one had to have the prisoners make some space. They were a remarkably cheerful bunch, however, and we lost the match by three goals to two—a satisfying, and diplomatically safe, result.

It was said that sometimes a man who would gain international notoriety turned up to watch the boxers. That was the aforementioned Idi Amin. He would have been in his late thirties at the time, and it has been claimed that he was the heavyweight boxing champion of Uganda some years earlier. He had spent sixteen years in the British army and had been a favorite of theirs. He claimed that no one had ever beat him in the boxing ring, but there was no verification of that, and when he was in power, it was not a good idea to challenge that claim. A few years' after I had left the country, and Idi had overthrown the government, he declared himself president. He then became a ruthless dictator and went on to destroy his country. One of his henchmen was an English guy named Bob Astles, who had founded a small aviation company. I took a flight from Kampala to Mwanza in one of Bob's planes, a six-seater De Haviland, I think. Astles himself was the pilot. While flying over Lake Victoria, I looked up from reading the newspaper to see that he, instead of looking where he was going, was also reading the newspaper. It was not a reassuring sight.

In early 1964, there were some small-scale uprisings in the Ugandan army. A barracks was seized and some army officers detained. President Obote got nervous and called on some units of the British army who were stationed in East Africa, to restore order. This did not go down well, as Uganda was by then independent of Britain, and many resented the involvement of British soldiers. However, after a couple of days, things settled down and the Ugandan and British soldiers decided to stage a boxing match. It was held at the police athletic grounds in Kampala, and the venue was packed with enthusiastic and noisy supporters. It was a wild affair. In one particular contest, the Ugandan boxer knocked the British soldier down with his first punch, but the British guy got up and knocked the Ugandan down. They took turns knocking each other down for three rounds, and the crowd roared its approval. The judges wisely declared the match a draw, and both boxers received cheers and great applause. There was genuine sportsmanship between the Ugandan boxers and the British soldiers, and it might have gone some way toward assuaging lingering resentments.

When I left Uganda to return to England in late 1964, all seemed well. Life was pleasant, and the future looked good.

It was some time after I had returned to England that Idi Amin seized power, and things took a turn for the worse. He expelled persons of Asian descent, and many of the Europeans followed of their own accord. Fortunately, that era passed. Today, the beautiful country of Uganda prospers, and Kampala is highly recommended as a good town to live in and to visit. It was my favorite town in East Africa, and one of the most wonderful places I have ever lived in.

RONNIE MANSFIELD AND THE INCOMPETENT MISTER

A Disastrous Medical Experience

ONNIE MANSFIELD LIVED ONLY A FEW BLOCKS away from and me in Peckham. We knew each other through the Boy Scouts. Like me, Ronnie had failed his eleven-plus examination and gone to a dead-end school, but he was smart enough. He gave the outward impression of being somewhat child-like, but there was something genuine and deep about him. He was thoughtful about what he said and careful when he gave an opinion. He had a keen interest in the medical profession and volunteered to do orderly work at New Cross Hospital. He wheeled patients to where they needed to be and did whatever the nursing staff asked him to. He liked to talk to the patients and do what he could for them. While busy at his jobs, he tried to learn all he could. He listened and watched. He listened to the instructions given to the nurses, and, by the doctors, to the medical students. He watched as patients were prepared for surgery. I don't know how much he learned, but it was enough to be very wary of doctors.

Sometime in the early 1950s, while playing football for Brixton School of Building, I suffered a bad injury to my right knee. I was tripped and, with the studs in my right boot embedded in the soil and anchoring my foot to the ground, I fell, pivoting around the knee.

It felt like a stick of celery being twisted. I knew it was bad. The knee swelled up like an enormous balloon and was so painful that I could not walk for some days. Eventually, I managed to get out of the house and hobble down Lausanne Road to Queens Road in Peckham, to see Dr. Purser. There were no set appointments to see the doctor; it was a bit like going for a haircut—you noted who was ahead of you and waited your turn. When mine came, I showed my knee to the doctor and tried to convey to him how it had happened and how much more swollen it had been three days before. He gave me a note to take to New Cross Hospital to have an x-ray. The hospital technician was Dr. Purser's son. He took the x-ray, told me, "No bones broken," and that was that.

In the 1950s, there was no way an x-ray could show soft tissue, and knee cartilage is soft tissue. Today, a dye can be injected into whatever joint needs to be looked at, and any damage can be seen on the x-ray.

I could not play football again; I wore a knee bandage and got around as best I could, but the difficulties with the knee got worse. I went back to Dr. Purser and managed to get another note, this time to be examined by a specialist, so returned to New Cross Hospital. The specialist was Mr. Lawson—not Doctor Lawson, because he was a surgeon. British surgeons, in their own minds, were so far above ordinary medical people that they rejected the title of doctor.

They had to be addressed as Mister. Lawson in particular had a colossal opinion of himself. He looked at my knee and thought that I might have a torn cartilage, a very common injury among footballers, and that the best thing to do was to have an operation. He taught at Guy's Hospital, a famous teaching hospital in south London. He wanted a knee operation to demonstrate to his students how to remove a cartilage, whether it needed to be removed or not. I was the guinea pig.

A date was set for me to be admitted. I would have to be in for ten days or more because the healing process would take a long time. I was admitted and given a bed, and soon became aware of who the important people in a hospital were. Above all, there was the matron. She was in charge of all the nursing staff in the hospital, and everyone trembled before her, even the most senior medical people. As for the ward sister, she was totally in charge of her ward. She shouted at, and verbally abused, the medical students and nurses in her charge. I remember the sister in charge of my ward shouting at a medical student, "Get out of the way, you fool." The poor young fellow got out of the way as fast as his legs would allow him. I soon learned that when the matron, or the ward sister, came around, it was best to lie at attention in bed and not ask any questions.

The nursing staff were under stern supervision, more for the benefit of the matron than the patients. They spanned the social classes, had working-and middle-class backgrounds, and some even hailed from the so-called upper classes. A number of the latter came from very well-to-do and titled, families. They had been sent to schools that did not have high academic requirements but cost a lot of money to go to. The intent was for them to become proper young ladies. They went to finishing school in Switzerland, and some would even be presented to the Queen as débutantes. I think this had something to do with providing an opportunity for eligible bachelors to have a look at them.

None of this made them smarter or better than the nurses from working-class backgrounds. They had affected accents and an over-the-top way of speaking, but they were kind and did their jobs. Some of the cockney patients would mock them with outrageous impersonations of their affected English, and the poor nurses could not reply. The young nurses generally lived in hostels and were under firmly enforced curfew rules: No hanging out with the young lads at night. They were brought to the hospital for their work shift in buses; the outgoing shift would board the same buses and be taken back to the hostel. When one thinks of a 1950s English nurse, one thinks of starch. Their uniforms were impeccable: spotless aprons and wonderful little hats that somehow managed to remain attached to their heads.

Hospital visiting hours were very restricted. You had to be in your bed when the bell rang to let in the visitors, and they had to get out quickly when the bell rang to announce that visiting hours were over.

Ronnie Mansfield did come to see me before the operation. He told me that, if the surgeon could not determine, before he made an incision, if it was the inside or the outside cartilage that was torn, then he should be prepared to look at both sides of the knee. He also told me that I was in the wrong hospital. "You should be in New Cross," he said. "That's the place for knee operations."

I really didn't know what I could do. I, like most other folks at that time, thought that doctors were brilliant people. We thought they knew what they were doing, and that we helpless patients should not question or challenge their judgments.

The day before my operation, Mr. Lawson came around, followed by a bunch of very young-looking medical students who were clearly in awe of him. The ward sister and several nurses were there, including the nurse assigned to me, the Honorable Wendy, I forget her last name. She was from a noble family and had indeed been presented, as a débutante, to The Queen, which meant she was ready to move into the upper echelons of society. She was very beautiful, somewhat like Julie Christy as Lara in *Dr. Zhivago*. Also, she was warm and friendly.

Lawson launched into his presentation. He said that some famous surgeon of years gone by, Sir somebody or other, would begin his day by performing half a dozen of these knee operations to "warm up before he got to the real stuff."

I should have walked out then.

He then tried to determine which side of the knee had been damaged by the maneuver called, if I remember right, the Murphy maneuver. He twisted the knee in all directions to elicit a click from the damaged cartilage. He could not get a click. Then he made this amazing statement: "It is usually the inside one."

I thought then of what Ronnie Mansfield had told me about examining both sides of the knee. I should have asked the obvious question—if it turned out that it wasn't the inside one, then what? But I didn't. I was intimidated by that fool of a surgeon. On the day of the operation, I was given an anesthetic and wheeled into the operation room.

The anesthetic that was used in the 1950s had a strange effect on patients. The patient in the next bed to me came out of his stupor singing bawdy ballads and old music hall songs. The whole ward tuned in to listen to his songs. I came around feeling very amorous towards the nearest nurse, who turned out to be an attractive, and pleasantly buxom, young woman from Wales. She was talking me back into the world in her lovely Welsh accent. As the muscle around my knee had been cut through, my leg was wasted and as skinny as a stick. The muscle had to be rebuilt. This meant about eight or nine days in hospital with lots of muscle-building exercises.

I wanted to see the report on the operation; I knew it was in the folder hanging at the foot of the bed. However, the contents of the report were only for the eyes of medical personnel. Patients were forbidden to look at them on pain of something terrible happening to them, but in the middle of the night, and with a friendly night nurse, it was easily done. Luckily for me, the Hon. Wendy was my night nurse. The report said that the inside cartilage had been removed, and that there was no sign of any damage. The idiot Mr. Lawson had removed a perfectly good cartilage from my knee, and left the torn one in.

About thirty years later, with the introduction of arthroscopic surgery, I had the offending cartilage removed from the outside of the knee by a brilliant surgeon in New Jersey. The American surgeon, who did not have to be addressed as Mister, described the damage as a "large bucket-handle tear." Maybe the distance between doctor and patient was always wider in the UK than in the U.S.A., or it could be that, in Mr. Lawson, I'd been unfortunate enough to have found an arrogant medical person of blinding incompetence.

That old knee still gives me problems. When I am riding my bike up what seems to me to be a steep hill, and feel the stabbing twinges, the dreaded Lawson comes to mind.

I did see my night nurse, Wendy, again, we went out to dinner somewhere in London. She was, indeed, very lovely. Sometime later, I received a postcard from Austria, where she was on a skiing trip with her wealthy mum and dad. As for the handsome and buxom nurse I woke up to, well, a month or so after the hospital stay, I bumped into her at the London Welsh Club, in the Greys Inn Road. She had come for the Saturday night dance, as had I. It turned out we were both Saturday night dance regulars.

What became of Ronnie Mansfield, I don't know. I hope he found some success and happiness. He was a good and sincere fellow. He did not have the schooling of Mr. Lawson, but he was so much wiser.

AN EMBARRASSING SPELLING MISTAKE, AND THE MIGHTY ATOM

A Story of Track and Field

SYDNEY CHARLES WOODERSON, *aka* "The Mighty Atom," was Britain's premier middle-distance runner in the 1930s and 1940s. When I was a schoolboy, Wooderson was one of my heroes, and in the 1960s, through being a member of an athletics club called the Deptford Park Harriers, I would get to meet him.

At five foot six inches tall and 123 pounds, with thick-lensed, horn-rimmed eyeglasses, Wooderson did not cut an imposing figure, yet he was one of the most fearsome track racers of his time. He ran in the days when track and field athletes were true amateurs. They had jobs. They trained during lunch hours and in the evenings. On weekends, they would compete for their clubs and paid their own way to do so. Wooderson also had his legal studies to contend with.

A sprained ankle ruined Sydney's chances at the 1936 Berlin Olympic Games, but in those pre-World War II years he set world records in the mile, half mile, and 800 meters. He was twice a European champion—in Paris in 1938, at 1,500 meters; and in Oslo in 1946, at 5,000 meters. In Oslo, he beat the track immortal Emil Zatopek and the great Belgian Gaston Reiff. I remember sitting on the edge of my chair, listening to the radio broadcast of that race. The voice of the commentator rose with excitement when Wooderson took the lead and, with a blistering finish, won going away in the second fastest time ever.

Like so many of his contemporaries, he lost what would have been his greatest years to the Second World War. Poor eyesight kept him out of active service in the war, but he was in the army, and served with distinction on the home front as a firefighter during the Blitz, and as a radar operator.

After the war, Sydney came back to run his best-ever mile; then, after his victory in Oslo, it was expected that he would run for Britain in the 1948 London Olympic Games. He had already won the British Cross-Country Championships that year so was in good form. But for some reason, he retired from international competition before the Games. He had to watch as the 5,000 meters was won by Gaston Reiff, setting a new Olympic record, followed by Zatopek and Slijkhuis of the Netherlands. Two years earlier, in Oslo, Sydney had left these three trailing in the dust with a much faster winning time.

The 1948 London Olympic Games were amazing. Just three years after the end of the war, with Europe still in disarray and much of London in ruins, it was a daunting task for Britain to host the Games. The odds against success were great, but the Games turned out to be splendid. It was a time of austerity, so the budget was small—athletes brought their own towels, were billeted in old army

Sydney Wooderson

huts, and traveled by the London Underground to get to their events, but enthusiasm was high.

The world was pulling its socks up and preparing to move forward again. The Games would be a great start. Twelve years had passed since the last games in Berlin, and after the six- year trauma of the war, the public was eager for something to celebrate. Eighty thousand people filled the stands at Wembley Stadium on a glorious, sun-drenched day. They had come to see King George declare the Games open and to watch the parade of athletes from around the globe assemble in the stadium. The highlight would be seeing the final torch bearer run one lap of the track, then light the Olympic flame.

It was considered a no-brainer that the retired Sydney Wooderson would be given the honor of being the final torch bearer and the one to light the flame. He was, after all, still one of the most famous runners in the world and he was Britain's great champion.

It is commonly accepted, that the British Olympic Committee *did* let Wooderson believe that he would be the torch bearer and the one to light the flame, and he had set about preparing for the occasion. Then, at the very last moment, he was told that the honor would go to someone else. The truth is, the Olympic Committee had chosen the final torch bearer some months earlier but had kept it a secret. They wanted it to be a surprise. Their intent was that the final torch bearer would bring to mind a classic Greek athlete—tall, statuesque, and with a regal stride. They wanted the lighting of the flame to be a glorious and dramatic sight, and indeed, it was.

The chosen runner was magnificent. Wooderson would not have looked so good, but he did deserve the honor. Sadly, it seems, he had been deceived by an Olympic Committee that included Harold Abrahams, of *Chariots of Fire* movie fame, and Lord Burghley. They were both Olympic champions, and they must have known in their hearts, that Sydney Wooderson should have been the athlete to light the Olympic flame.

Only a few trivia buffs will remember the name of the final torch bearer, John Mark. He was a very decent fellow and a good 400-

meter runner. He ran for Cambridge University and did win an England vest, running the 400 meters against France. He was also an excellent Rugby player. He studied medicine and became a much beloved doctor in the county of Hampshire. His final lap run to open the games at Wembley was dramatic and inspiring, just what the organizers wanted. When he entered the stadium, he stopped at the edge of the track and raised the torch high above his head, and then, with a classic stride, circled the Wembley track in front of that mighty crowd and the Olympic competitors who were gathered in the infield. On reaching the cauldron that would hold the flame, he again stopped and raised the torch high for all the crowd to see. He then lit the flame. It was a beautiful sight, and it must have been a heady moment for John Mark. However, at the time, and among aged runners and track historians today, the opinion remains that the honor of lighting the 1948 Olympic Flame should have gone to Sydney Wooderson.

Some fifteen years after those London games, Deptford Park Harriers, the track and field club I belonged to, decided to host a track and field meeting, and to invite clubs in the London area to compete. Deptford lies on the south bank of the Thames in South East London and has a place in history. It is the site of the savage murder of the playwright Christopher Marlow, a contemporary of William Shakespeare, and Sir Francis Drake sailed his ship, the *Golden Hind,* in to Deptford Creek in 1581. In the late 1690s, Russia's Peter the Great came to Deptford to study the art of ship building.

In the late nineteenth century, the borough fathers converted a market garden into a seventeen-acre park. They named it Deptford Park. Well, why not? Later, a full-sized cinder running track was added. Then, in the mid-1950s, a former schoolmate of mine, Bernard Smith, chose this track to be the home of Deptford Park Harriers, a club made up of a bunch of athletes Bernard had gathered together. It was a small club, with no coach and only cold-water showers, but it had some very fine and interesting athletes. In 1962, this group settled on the very ambitious project of presenting a grand track and field contest, and they wanted a great name to be associated with the venture. They did not have to look far.

Sydney Wooderson was a local lad, and needless to say a hero to every member of Deptford Park Harriers. He was also an inspiration to Roger Bannister, the first athlete to run the mile in under four minutes. Wooderson was born, and lived, not far from Deptford Park, so some lads from the club approached the great man to ask if the Harriers could have the honor of naming their tournament the "Sydney Wooderson Trophy Meeting." They told Sydney that they would raise the money to buy a silver cup, have his name engraved on it, and present it to the club that won the competition. He agreed and said he would be happy to attend the event and to award the cup.

April, was the month chosen for the great competition, a bit early in the year for a Track & Field meeting. It was a damp and chilly day and the sky was overcast, with a threat of rain, not an unusual day in an English spring. The scoring for the event was to follow what was known as the Portuguese system, which in essence meant that everyone who competed would score points for his or her club. On the day of the competition, many London area clubs had gathered for the event, and to honor Sydney Wooderson. The Deptford Park Harriers' own miler, Bill Giddings, was there; he had not long before, on a very rough cinder track and on a wet and windy day, run the mile in 4 minutes and 3.5 seconds. This was faster than Sydney's best. Bill had the potential for greatness.

True to his word, Sydney Wooderson turned up at the track, still

Following in the footsteps of Sydney Wooderson, the Deptford Park miler Bill Giddings wins the Surrey mile in 1960.

looking trim and fit. He wore a raincoat but was bare headed. There were a few chairs set up alongside the back straight of the track where Sydney could sit and watch the events if he wanted to, but he wanted to be involved, he wanted something to do, so he volunteered to be a timekeeper. This bowled the Deptford Park guys over, and after a brief meeting, they gave him the job of chief time-keeper.

The trophy, a tall silver cup, stood on a table, waiting to be awarded to the club that earned the most points. At one point, when he wasn't working as a timekeeper, Sydney walked over to take a look at the cup that had been named in his honor. He picked it up and turned it round to read the inscription. Then he said, "You have spelt my name wrong."

No one knew what to say, but the engraving read *SIDNEY* instead of *SYDNEY*. It was a great embarrassment for all. Why had no one thought to call and ask him how he would like his name to be spelled? Still, the meet went on, and Sydney Wooderson graciously presented the cup to the winning club, Walton A.C., then went home.

I am not sure how many subsequent runnings for the Sydney Wooderson Trophy there were, but I know it was more than a one-off affair. Where is the cup today? No one seems to know. Hopefully, it stands proudly on someone's mantelpiece. Perhaps in years to come it will turn up, and the finder maybe be moved to find out more about the great Sydney Wooderson and the sport of Track & Field.

In spite of the embarrassing spelling mistake, Deptford Park Harriers made a better effort to honor, and show respect for Sydney Wooderson, South East London's pride, than had the 1948 British Olympic committee.

Sydney was finally honored in the year 2000, for his services to athletics. He was made a Member of the British Empire, even though there was no longer an empire. A kind and unassuming man, he was totally loyal to his club, the Blackheath Harriers, throughout his life. He died in 2006 at the age of ninety-two and is buried in the churchyard of Lady Saint Mary's Church, Wareham, in the beautiful County of Dorset.

Endnote

In the 1952 Olympic Games, the Finns honored their track great, Parvo Nurmi, by having him carry the torch into the stadium and light the flame. In the 1940s, Alan Turing, the mathematician, instrumental in breaking the Enigma code in World War II, was a member of Walton AC. He was shortlisted for the 1948 games as a marathon runner. His story is told in the Oscar nominated movie The Imitation Game. Harold Abrahams was the 100-meter Olympic champion in Paris, 1924, and Lord Burghley was the 400-meter hurdles Olympic Champion in Amsterdam, 1928.

THE PROGRAM SELLER AND QUEEN SALOTE

Coronation Day

JUNE 2, 1953, WAS A WET AND WINDY DAY in London Town. It was also unseasonably cold. Not that unseasonable weather is uncommon in London; it occurs as often as what they call seasonable weather. What can be said is that June 2 was damp, chilly, and miserable. On any other day the weather would not have been of much concern, but that was the day that had been chosen for the coronation of Queen Elizabeth II. She'd actually become Queen eighteen months earlier, on the day her father, King George VI died. To make it official, however, there had to be a coronation. It had to be formally declared to the world that Elizabeth was, "by the Grace of God, of Great Britain, Ireland, and the British Dominions beyond the seas, Queen." She would also become "Defender of the Faith," a title inherited from King Henry VIII, who claimed the designation for himself when he severed ties with the Pope in Rome. Severing was quite a pastime for Henry. "Queen of Ireland" was a bit of a stretch: That also dated back to King Henry. Maybe Queen of the North East corner of Ireland would have been better.

Coronation Day had been decided on by a committee formed to organize the whole show. They had to settle on the date a year ahead of time and hope for the best—and for good weather. Weather was important, as an enormous procession through the streets of London was planned, and the crowd was expected to rise into the millions.

In a bizarre move, the committee asked the weather forecasting folks to look up the historical records, and to settle a date upon which it was least likely to rain. A crystal ball would have served just as well. The records indicated that June 2 had the best chance of acceptable weather, so that's what they chose. On the auspicious day, it drizzled, it rained, and it poured. So much for historical records. They must have been a bunch of crackpots to even try to forecast what the weather would be like a year ahead of time. English weather changes every ten minutes.

June 1 was fine, and the evening was good enough for people to pick their spots on the procession route and sleep out on the pavements. The morning of June 2, however, brought a dramatic change for the worse. The weather folks said it was high pressure over the Atlantic and low pressure over Europe, or maybe it was the other way round—who knows. Whatever it was, it was the cause of the terrible weather.

To help with chores on the big day—selling souvenir programs, opening car doors, and so on—the organizers recruited boy scouts and young people from similar groups. I was by then eighteen years old, and my active scouting days were nearly over, but I was still involved with the scouts to some extent, as an assistant scout leader. Knowing that it was going to be a long day, the organizers wanted older volunteers, which included scouts, for many chores. It sounded like an opportunity to be a part of history; that might be overstating it a bit, but I decided to do it.

So on the evening of June 1, I put on my old scouts uniform and reported to County Hall, on the south side of Westminster Bridge, where I would learn about the responsibilities of being a program seller. County Hall was the headquarters of the London County Council, and one of the centers of operations on Coronation Day. Volunteers were allowed to stay in County Hall on the night of June 1. I can't recall what the sleeping arrangements were, but they had to have been a lot better than sleeping outside on the cold concrete pavement, which hundreds of thousands of spectators were doing.

At about 6:00 a.m. on the morning of June 2, I left County Hall and walked across Westminster Bridge to the prime sales territory that had been assigned to me. It was in Parliament Square, near Westminster Abbey. I had a bunch of souvenir programs in a bag slung over my shoulder, and a tin with a slot in the top for taking money. The programs were to be sold for half a crown—that is, two shillings and sixpence—each. It had not started to rain yet, but it did not look good. The gray light of dawn was made darker by the threatening skies, but spirits were high among people who had slept out all night in order to get a good position to see the Queen, and the great procession.

Viewing stands had been built in Parliament Square, and those who had reserved seats had to be in those seats very early in the morning and then stay within the confines of the viewing area. Hope they had plenty of Porta-Potties. It must have been uncom-

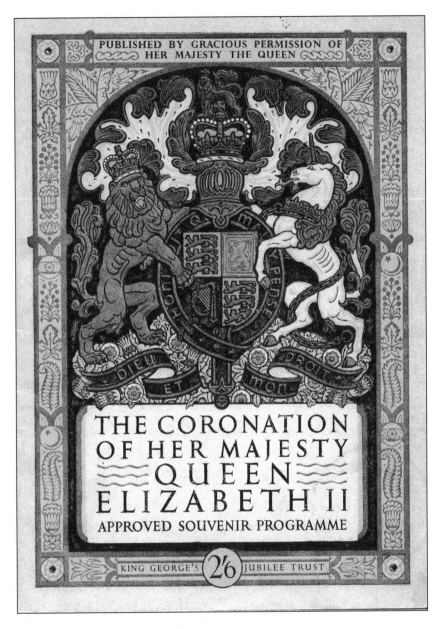

The Coronation Program

fortable, but the people still seemed happy. I don't know why the police were so strict in not allowing them to move around, as this was many hours before the arrival of the Queen, and it seemed absurd that nobody could cross the street. I have since found out that that is just the way it is with parades and the police. The latter just don't like people crossing streets; they want them to stay in place.

In the early hours of the morning, excitement began rippling through the crowd as the news came that Edmund Hillary and Tiger Tenzing Norgay had reached the summit of Mount Everest. They were the first climbers to have conquered the mountain and safely returned to their base camp. Edmund, later Sir Edmund, was quoted as saying: "We knocked the bastard off." It seemed like a good omen for Queen Elizabeth on her big day.

Unlike the trapped spectators, I was free to go where I liked. I saw the first soldiers line the route around the square. They stood about three feet apart, each having placed his neatly folded rain gear at his feet. When the rain began, I expected someone in command to tell the soldiers to put the gear on, but no one did. I watched the soldiers' uniforms turn from damp to sodden as the rain soaked into the fabric of their clothing. But they had to endure the absurdity and discomfort of their situation. They must above all not move, of course— only an officer could tell them to do that. I can't recall seeing any officers, but they must have been somewhere nearby.

I found shelter under the awnings around the Abbey. Lords, dukes, and earls, with finely attired ladies, all in their ceremonial gear, were huddled in similar places. It was like they were taking a tea break. Some had loosened their robes and rolled their trousers up, as one would to go paddling in the ocean. They were showing off their fancy ceremonial socks, many of them puffing cigarettes. Not an impressive looking lot at all.

After the invited congregation of musicians, choirs, and dignitaries had assembled in the Abbey, the real guests of honor came in. Not many Londoners knew who these guests of honor were, and neither did I; they were of little interest. The crowd was waiting for the Queen.

She eventually arrived in an enormous golden horse-drawn coach, attended by costumed footmen and the oddly named Household Cavalry. She was assisted out of the coach, and she needed all the assistance she could get, as she was wearing her coronation outfit, which included the heavy, cumbersome Robe of State. It was almost too much for her. The Queen was quoted as saying to her attendants: "Give me a push to get me started." She then had to drag the twelve-foot-long robe up the carpeted aisle, to where the Archbishop of Canterbury was waiting for her. It has been reported that the pile of the carpet was against her, and the friction between the robe and carpet more than doubled her task.

The ceremony was covered on TV, the commentator being the well-known Richard Dimbleby. He spoke in hushed and reverent whispers as he described the rituals of the coronation in the Abby. His commentary was broadcast to the crowd in the square, and, I think, to everyone with a wireless in Britain.

One part of the ceremony was not shown to the public. That was the "mystery of the Anointing," when the Archbishop touched the Queen with oils. To quote from the order of service, "Four Knights of the Garter, in their velvet mantles of azure lined in white, hold over her a canopy of cloth of gold, so that she is fully seen by none but the Archbishop." The Archbishop then dips his thumb into a spoon filled with consecrated oils and "touches the Queen on her hands, her breast, and the crown of her head." That must have been a heady moment for his Aged Eminence, but he seems to have held it together.

And that was the story. The Queen at that time was a very attractive young woman, and whether the elderly cleric followed all of the instructions as written we shall never know. It was a long and tiring ceremony, and the language was archaic—at one point the Archbishop prays for the Queen to use the Sword of State for the "terror and punishment of evildoers," not easy listening for those outside in the rain who could not see what was going on inside the Abbey. Keeping out of the rain took precedence over listening to the Archbishop droning on. So I returned to one of the dry spots under an awning around the Abbey.

When the Queen had been crowned and all of the formalities were over, it was time to head back to Buckingham Palace. The Abbey bells clanged and clanged, and the crowds lining the streets were ready to see the mighty procession pass by on its long and circuitous journey back to the palace. It was probably the last great parade of its kind that the world would ever see. It was said to be three miles long, with bands, mounted soldiers, foot soldiers, sailors, and airmen from all over what was still known as the British Empire, on which the sun was about to set. There were scores of magnificent horse-drawn carriages carrying very important people, and a lot of people no one had ever heard of, like the Sultan of Selangor. Where is Selangor? There was, however, among the famous and the nobodies, a clear superstar apart from the Queen herself—someone most people in Britain had never heard of.

Queen Salote Mafile'o Pilolevu Tupou III of Tonga, generally known as Queen Salote, stole the show. She was a very very large woman, six feet three inches tall, they said, and she weighed in at more than three hundred pounds. She had a reputation in Tonga as a writer of dance songs and love poems, and she won the hearts of the crowd and all of London. She was greeted as the tallest queen of the smallest kingdom, and she clearly meant to enjoy her special moment in the pouring rain. She wanted to connect with the crowd, and connect she did. She refused to have the hood drawn over her open carriage and chose instead to brave the wet and windy elements. Hers was the only open carriage in the parade. She laughed and waved with great vigor, and just enjoyed herself. The British people were not used to royal folks being animated and appearing to be openly happy. Before Queen Salote, a royal wave had been no more than a slight turning of the hand. In fact, it still is.

The crowd loved and responded to the splendid and animated queen. Her companion in the carriage, however, did not. He was a small, sad, and huddled figure in a tall white hat—His Highness the Sultan of Kelantan. Kelantan is somewhere in Malaysia, and that is all I know about it. He huddled tightly in the carriage, as though he were trying to wrap himself around himself to keep warm. He wanted to be somewhere else, out of the rain, but the poor fellow had to put up with his situation for the length of the parade route. He may have been a big shot in Kelantan, but he wasn't going to tell the Queen of Tonga what to do.

After the coronation, Edmundo Ros, the leader of a South American orchestra in Britain, recorded a song, written by Jack Fishman, called "The Queen of Tonga." It became very popular. It was not quite Cole Porter, but it was a good, easy-to-sing pub number with a sing-along chorus:

And when the people saw her on that torrential morn,
She captured all before her, took everyone by storm.

Chorus:

The Queen of Tonga came to Britain from far away,
The Queen of Tonga came to Britain on Coronation Day.

When the celebrated singer, composer, and cabaret performer Noel Coward was asked if he knew who the small man in the carriage with the Tongan Queen was, he replied, "Her lunch." It should be noted, however, that the very small sultan had three wives and twenty-three children, so, maybe he was a bit of a dark horse.

Once the parade had passed, the party was over. I did not feel like going to Buckingham Palace to stand in the crowd and wait for the Queen to come out onto the balcony, so I walked back to County Hall to hand in my unsold programs. Had I sold any, I would have had to hand in some money, and though I do not recollect selling even one, I must have, sold at least two or three. But it escapes me.

Having finished my program-selling duties, I left County Hall, strolled to the bus stop, and waited for a bus to take me back to Peckham. I think the weather had improved a little by the evening, and the street parties were still going on when I got back to Lausanne Road. Many streets, all over the country, had been closed to vehicular traffic to enable people to have parties, and like everyone else in the country, the people of Peckham had spent the day listening to the broadcast on the radio, or, if they were lucky, huddled around a small black-and-white television set with their neighbors. They had tables and chairs set up in the street, and they partied. They ate, drank, danced, sang, and got rained on, but it didn't seem to matter; you get rained on a lot in London.

LENNY, FRANK, AND HILDERGARDE

Music-Making in New York City

L ENNY METCALF PLAYED THE PIANO in New York City. It was how he made his living. He came from England to America through being a band leader on an oceangoing liner, the *Mauretania*, I think it was. The liner docked in New York harbor and sometime in the 1950s; Lenny got off the ship, stayed in the city, and became a New Yorker. I did once ask him what had led him to leave the ship, give up a good job, and try his luck in the city. He said that there might have been a young lady in the picture. Lenny was a tall, handsome, and charismatic Londoner who became a fixture in New York's piano bar scene. So many in the field of entertainment knew Lenny, and they came to hear him play. He became the quintessential New Yorker, but, in his heart, he remained a Londoner. He often said, "You can always tell a Londoner, but you can't tell him much."

I met Lenny through being in a production of the Gershwin musical *Of Thee I Sing* at Symphony Space, a beloved New York City institution. There was an English singer named Bridget in the show. She also sang with an English music hall group known as the London Pearlies, an ensemble led by the piano player—Lenny Metcalf. Bridget thought I would enjoy meeting Lenny and his team, so she took me along to a performance. She was right. The London Pearlies were the real thing. Great songs and singers, jokes by James, and showmanship. Bridget introduced me to Lenny, a fellow Londoner, and I liked him right away. He invited me to try my luck as a Pearly.

I became a member of the group a bit late in the day, as the Pearlies had been around for awhile and built up a sterling reputation and a strong following. However, when I *did* join, I got to wear a splendid pearly outfit that was fashioned after the suits worn by the Pearly Kings and Queens of London. The suits were made by sewing many hundreds of pearl buttons onto jackets, trousers, dresses, and flamboyant hats. The hats for the ladies were spectacular.

The Pearlies had gigs at venues throughout the city, the Armory on Park Avenue, the English-Speaking Union on Madison Avenue, and at various pubs and clubs. They sang for associations of British war brides (there were still plenty of those in the 1980s) and for St. George's Day, where we became very patriotic and always remembered to toast the Queen. There were special concerts to commemorate events and battles of the world wars. The celebration of the Battle of Britain was an enormous occasion, and there was always a big turnout for that. Lenny, like me, had been a wartime evacuee from London during World War II. He was fortunate in that he had been billeted in the fine county of Cambridgeshire with people who cared for him. At the fiftieth anniversary of the Battle of Britain, in

1990, he traveled back to England for the celebrations and stayed with the then-very elderly folks who had been his foster parents during the war. He said that some of the happiest times of his life were the years spent with those Cambridgeshire folks, as an evacuee.

Many years ago, sometime in the 1980s, I had a gig with Lenny at the Seventh Regiment Armory on Park Avenue. The Armory is a mighty and very famous historic building in the City; it fills an entire city block between Park and Lexington Avenues. The event was the annual remembrance of the Battle of Britain, and we had a good, and mostly British, audience. We were joined for the performance by an Irish-American named Frank McCourt, then a teacher in the New York City School system. I had never met Frank before, but I had met his brother, Malachy, a well-known character actor in the New York City theater scene. Frank and I were dressed in World War II British army uniforms, complete with tin hats, while Lenny, at the piano, wore his tuxedo.

Accompanied by Lenny, Frank and I traded songs from the 1930s and 1940s, and although I can't remember what we sang on that night, there are some really good songs from World Wars I & II—"Pack Up Your Troubles in Your Old Kit Bag," "The White Cliffs of Dover," and many more. The closer was always "We'll Meet Again," a Vera Lynn classic that just about everyone of a certain age would know. The audience joined in on every chorus, and Lenny added a couple of his own inimitable Music Hall classics. "Maybe It's Because I'm A Londoner" was a favorite.

At some point in the show, Lenny recognized a very famous entertainer in the audience. She was accompanied by a high-ranking military person, and Lenny invited her up to sing. It is possible that he knew that she would be in the audience and had prearranged with her to sing a song, but I don't know that. She was extremely elegant, and, although not young, was very glamorous. She stepped up to the front of the performing area, and Lenny introduced her to the audience with just one name. *Hildegarde!* There she stood in person. She was among the first of many entertainers to go by one name, and in the 1930s and '40s, she was one of the most famous cabaret artists in the world. A native of Wisconsin, she was a legend in her own time, often being introduced as "The Incomparable Hildergarde." When speaking of her, the flamboyant pianist Liberace, also from Wisconsin, said that she was perhaps the most famous supper club entertainer who ever lived. It was Hildergarde's example that led Liberace to perform using a single name—a good thing, as Wladziu Valentino Liberace, was a bit of a mouthful. (To add a piece of trivia, a person who uses only one name is known as a "mononymous" person.)

Hildergarde had graced the finest cabarets and supper clubs in the world, and here she was at the Battle of Britain concert, in the New York Armory, with Lenny Metcalf, Frank McCourt, and me. I forget the name of the song she chose to sing, but her signature song was: "Darling, *Je Vous Aimee Beaucoup, Je Ne Sais Pas* What To Do," a mixture of French and English phrases. Hildergarde was an outstanding piano player in her own right and usually wore long white opera-length gloves, up to the elbows, while she accompanied herself. Maybe she forgot to bring her gloves with her on that night, but she was happy to have Lenny play for her. It was a wonderful and very special treat for us, and for the audience, and she was more than warmly applauded. I must admit that at that time, although I had known about Hildergarde many years before, she had faded in my memory, and I was not fully aware of her fame.

After the show, she—who apparently, always went around with her own photographer—said that she wanted to have some photographs taken with Frank and me in our World War II army uniforms. Her female photographer picked a spot in one of the hallways, set Hildergarde between the two of us, and took several photos from different angles. When she had finished, that was that. Frank and I changed into our street clothes, said good night, and went our separate ways home.

I never saw Frank McCourt, or Hildergarde, again, but a couple of years later, Frank came out with a mega-best-selling book called *Angela's Ashes*. It took the literary world by storm, winning a Pulitzer Prize, and becoming a *New York Times* number-one best-seller. It was an enormous success, and was eventually made into a movie.

In recent years, I have begun to wonder, even obsess, about the whereabouts of those photographs. It began to seem very significant, even, to some extent, historic. I have tried very hard to locate them, but I never knew the name of the photographer. Hildegarde died in 2006 at the age of ninety-nine, and Frank McCourt passed away in 2006, a month shy of his seventy-ninth birthday.

Several years ago, Lenny moved to the Victoria Home, a magnificent building in Ossining, New York, with enormous pictures of Queen Elizabeth, Queen Victoria, and other ancient and modern members of the British royal family hanging from the walls in heavy, ornate frames. The home, which is for men and women in their later years, is funded and managed by the Daughters of the British Empire. Some may be surprised to learn that there is such an organization, especially as there isn't any empire, but there they are, these Noble Daughters of the erstwhile Empire, who seem, at times, to have come from a different, gentler age. They manage four Victoria Homes throughout the U.S.A., and, by the looks of things, they manage them very well. They are kind and caring women, and they do good works. They are very patriotic, both to Britain and to their adopted country, the U.S.A. They gather to celebrate the special days of both nations and to sing the national songs. So, good for them, or, should I say, jolly good show.

I visited Lenny several times at the Victoria home. I did my best to pick a bright sunny day, and would call ahead to make sure all was well before driving north of the George Washington Bridge. On one occasion, I got there in time for afternoon tea. Since the day was warm and sunny, Lenny and I sat on the veranda, from which, if I remember correctly, there was a view of the Hudson River. A very nice woman (maybe she was a daughter of the empire) chatted with us for a while, and then asked if we would like a pot of tea. Musical words to any English person, and the answer, of course, was yes. So she brought us tea and some biscuits, (cookies, to Americans) served with china cups and plates of course. To be really English, there should have been cucumber sandwiches and Eccles cakes, but there you go, you can't have everything. The caregivers were very kind and clearly liked Lenny. We talked of his career, of his life in New York City, and of our time with the London Pearlies, and we sang old songs, always finishing with "We'll Meet Again."

Sadly, Lenny did not seem to be fully aware of his situation or to understand why he was where he was. He would say that he was "waiting for his people" to arrive, so that they could all go back to his apartment in lower Manhattan. His memory, however, for people, and events long gone by, was astounding. I listened to his recollections and was amazed at the details he could recall, and he was very clear in his memory of the evening with Frank and Hildergarde.

I last saw Lenny in the Victoria home in late October 2017. I had called ahead to make sure that he was up to receiving visitors, and then made the drive from New Jersey, across the George Washington Bridge, and then, a twenty-minute-or-so journey north to Ossining.

I checked in at the front desk and then took what must be the slowest elevator in the world up to Lenny's floor. He was sitting with some elderly folk in a small area used as a gathering place. A care worker was engaging some of the residents in an activity, and one old fellow was singing very loudly, and quite off key, into a microphone.

Lenny was asleep in his chair when I arrived. I sat for awhile until he appeared to be stirring, then said, "Hello, Lenny."

He opened his eyes, smiled, and said "Hello, David." He always remembered. To get away from the very loud and out-of-tune bellows of the singer, I wheeled Lenny to his own room, where we could chat. He told me how lucky he was to have a "lovely wife," and that he would be going home with her very soon. I asked him if he remembered the time when, at the New York Armory, Hildergarde sang for us and for Frank McCourt. He did, and he reminded me that she had been accompanied by some quite important military person. After awhile, I could see that Lenny was tiring, so we sang "We'll Meet Again," and then I took his hand and said, "Goodbye, Lenny."

"Goodbye, David," he said.

I went home, having admitted to myself that the quest to find the photograph with Frank and Hildergarde was over.

The importance of the work of Frank McCourt, and how incredible the story of Hildergarde was, eluded me at the time, but I know now that it is really too late to find a satisfactory ending for this story, and that all of it will eventually fade away. However, writing it has brought back fond memories of Lenny and the London Pearlies, and of singing English music hall songs in the pubs and clubs of New York. I could never have dreamed of doing that when I was a young lad growing up in South East London. So it was a good time, and a good quest.

An old musical joke is: How do you get to Carnegie Hall? The well-worn answer is: practice, practice, practice. Good saloon and barroom pianists, just like their classical brothers and sisters, have spent many hours and years practicing and honing their craft. They must be versatile, be able to sing and play the standards, the Great American Songbook, sing-alongs, and maybe a bit of ragtime here and there. The job has its difficulties, as there are sometimes noisy and indifferent audiences to deal with, and those who may have had a drop too much to drink. On the upside, there are the times when the room is totally with the piano player, and they merrily sing along and give loud applause. This is the great reward.

Lenny died near to Christmas in 2017. His "people" gathered at a restaurant on Washington Street on the Lower West Side of Manhattan to remember him. I think that his legacy is that, through his songs and piano playing, he helped to spread some joy. He liked people, and people liked him. How can you beat that for a winning combination? The wonderful Daughters of the British Empire looked after him until the end, they are good and devoted people.

How to finish but to say that at least you who have read this story will now know a little about the Victoria Homes, English afternoon teas, and Lenny Metcalf, piano player and Londoner.

THE SAD DEMISE OF THE PECKHAM HEALTH CENTER

NOT MANY PEOPLE IN LONDON had the opportunities offered to the people of Peckham by the Peckham Health Center. The brainchild of two medical doctors, George Scott Williamson and Innes Hope Pierce, The Center, as it was commonly called, was housed in a magnificent avant-garde building in St. Mary's Road, Peckham. Drs. Williamson and Pierce, who had a different approach to how medicine should be practiced, chose Peckham for their study. They chose the South East London borough because its population provided a good cross-section of the population of the nation as a whole. They signed up about a thousand families to form the membership of The Center, predominantly working- and middle-class families. The only way to become a member was to join as a family and to live in Peckham.

Drs. Williamson and Pierce led a team of doctors and social workers in researching what makes a community tick, and they dealt with the family as a unit. They studied health rather than disease.

The experiment started in 1926 and ended in 1950, when the financial burden of keeping the place up and running was proving difficult. Also, it did not align well with the medical approach of the National Health Service.

The Center was closed for the duration of the war, but it reopened in 1945, and that is when my family joined. It was the best thing we ever did as a family. It was an easy walk from our house in Lausanne Road, and the facilities were outstanding. The centerpiece was a magnificent swimming pool, with diving boards of specified Olympic height—ten and three meters—plus a springboard. It had a triangular glass roof to let in natural light, and windows running the full length of the pool on both sides to allow people to view the events in the pool. It is where I, and a number of my schoolmates, learned to swim.

There was a state-of-the-art gymnasium where I practiced the noble art of boxing. (I write about that in "Smith of Lambeth.") There were also two badminton courts, a fine theater for amateur dramatics, a well-stocked cafeteria near the swimming pool, a dance hall, snooker tables, and roller skating on the roof. There was even a farm in the country where Center members could practice organic farming.

Sadly, by 1950, financial hard times had begun to intrude on the Shangri-la that members of the Center had been enjoying since it reopened in 1945. The struggle to raise funds was becoming desperate. The doctors and managers of the Center had to persuade the folks who ran the National Health Service that the work they were doing was medically important.

In a last-gasp effort to save the facility from going broke, Drs. Williamson and Pierce appealed directly to the nation's Prime Minister, Clement Attlee, and to every mover and shaker they could find. They had to sell the merits of their approach to health care. To assist in their appeal, they hired a film company to make a short film to illustrate the Center's approach to family-based health care. The film was cast from members of the health center, and the chosen actors and the film were quite good. Anyone can see it today by going online.

The film showed at a local cinema, and many important people—and many others who just thought they were important— attended. The aged Queen Mary,[1] the grandmother of Queen Elizabeth II, was the great prize. The poor old dear was eighty-three at the time, but she was done up to the nines in the same Edwardian outfit she always wore. She dutifully tottered around the required tour of the facilities, looking totally bored. The prime minister, Clement Attlee, and his ministers, came to see the movie, none of them looking very excited to be there. Among the other invitees were a number of dubious but very rich socialites, most of whom were not of much use to anyone. I have a vague memory of that despot King Farouk of Egypt, and the Aga Khan, who weighed himself in gold every year, being there. I don't think the doctors would have got much out of those guys. Before the start of the movie, Dr. Williamson launched an appeal from the stage. He aimed his remarks directly at the Prime Minister and other government bigwigs, telling them how important the work of the health center was, and why they should give him lots of money to carry on with his work.

The members of the Center went about their normal routines while the VIPs were being shown around. I remember climbing out of the swimming pool and, through one of the glass windows that take up the two long sides of the pool, seeing the Queen Mother staring in at the swimmers. She looked very severe, and not at all amused.

The good doctors did not get the funds they needed. It seemed that their work, and their approach to medicine, did not fit in with the approach of the National Health Service, so, the Peckham Health Center had to close. The incredible building remained, of course, and was used thereafter by the local council for various social services and evening classes. It has now, so I have heard, been converted into apartments.

Drs. Williamson and Pierce eventually got married, at quite advanced ages. I don't know where they went, but their medical research at the center was over. The results and records of their experiments have, however, been recognized, and are still studied by many scholars and learned societies today.

I find it amazing, looking back to those post-war days of national austerity, that, in my working-class neighborhood, there was this incredible institution called The Peckham Health Center. It gave the residents of our borough so many opportunities for growth, discovery, and companionship. I can only look back with gratitude and thanks for the good doctors, George Scott Williamson, and Innes Hope Pierce.

Endnote

1. For those who like useless information, Queen Mary's full name was Victoria Mary Augusta Louise Olga Pauline Claudine Agnes. She was born in 1867.

GREENWICH PARK AND THE STRANGE SIGN IN THE POND

REENWICH PARK IS THE GLITTERING JEWEL of South East London. Close to the south bank of the Thames, it tightly hugs the maritime center of Greenwich at one end, and spreads its two hundred acres of green space and history up to Blackheath at the other. The two ends are divided by a very steep hill that, in years long gone by, was used for the dubious sport of mass tumbling—folks hurling themselves down the slope in a race to the bottom. This strange sport still survives in some parts of the country where the objective is to be the first to capture a rolling cheese, but it is no longer seen in Greenwich Park. Standing at the top of the hill, by the statue of General James Wolfe, hero of the battle of Quebec in 1759, a visitor has the most breathtaking views of London as it spreads out as far as the eye can see, like a gloriously colored quilt. Greenwich Park is a royal park, the oldest of eight such parks in London. I don't know why they're called "royal"; maybe they were once owned by the monarch, or, come to that, maybe they still are. It was not enclosed as a park until the sixteenth century, when King James I decided to have a twelve-feet-high brick wall built all around it. Earlier, King Henry VIII had kept a herd of deer in the park, but how he kept them in before James built the wall, I don't know. Descendants of those deer still roam the park today; they may not be direct descendants, but how could one possibly tell?

At the bottom of the hill sits the not-to-be-missed National Maritime Museum with its stories and exhibits of great sailors, explorers, and their ships, Admiral Horatio Nelson being the most famous of the sailors.

Among the trees in the park lie the sad remnants of a very ancient and once mighty oak. It is said to date back to the twelfth century. I saw it when I was very young, but it was barely recognizable as a tree even then, with its dead branches held up by many props. Now the dead remains sprawl on the ground, covered with fungus. In Henry VIII's reign, the tree lived, and it was a hollow tree—its historical interest came from claims that the young Queen Elizabeth 1 sat in its shade to eat and drink the sixteenth century equivalent of tea and cucumber sandwiches. Henry VIII is said to have danced around the tree with Anne Boleyn. Although it is not easy to imagine that very large Royal dancing, he was reputed to have been quite a sprightly fellow in his youth, and a *very* good dancer.

Even in Henry's day, the park had rules, and rule breakers were sometimes confined in the hollow part of the tree.

My parents met in the 1920s by the South Gates of this park, which open onto Blackheath. It was probably on a Sunday, when working folks had their leisure hours. Mum and Dad both lived on the Isle of Dogs, and they probably walked separately under the river, with family and friends, via the Greenwich Foot Tunnel, to Greenwich Pier, and then into the park. My mother was with some friends who knew Dad, and it was through this connection that they came to be introduced. A few years after that meeting, in 1928, they were married in Christ Church on the Isle of Dogs, on Christmas Day. It was not uncommon for working-class people to be married on that day. My family were all *Islanders*.

For visitors to Greenwich, walking through the foot tunnel is exciting. It was designed by an eminent civil engineer named Sir Alexander Bonnie, who was responsible for a number of river crossings. Construction of the tunnel began under Queen Victoria, and it opened in 1902 under Edward VII. Children like to run through the four hundred meters or so of passageway, although running is discouraged, and echoes of footsteps and laughing voices ring from one end of the tunnel to the other. When the ancient and clunky old lifts at each end break down, which occurs quite often, walkers must climb a hundred steps that circle around the lift shafts to get to street level.

The tunnel was an integral part of the lives of my family; it was their passage to and from Greenwich, where there was some entertainment, and it featured in many of their stories.

With my friends from the Deptford Park Harriers, I trained in the park for cross-country running. It was perfect for that, but for the most part the park was enjoyed for its beauty and serenity. A fine amateur cricket team, the West Kent Wanderers, played over the weekends and always brought a good number of cricket fans into the park. The spectators clapped politely and said things like, "Well played, sir." There was no shouting or singing at cricket matches in those days. It would have been extremely bad form.

The park, like all good English parks, boasts a very good tea room. It is near to the Observatory and to General Wolfe. Tea rooms are essential to good parks and to the British way of life, and this one does not disappoint. A pot of tea and an Eccles cake will complete any afternoon in a far more satisfying way than any offering in one of the fancy new-wave coffee shops. Near the tea rooms and General Wolfe stands the Royal Observatory and the Greenwich meridian, which separates east from west. This is a great attraction for tourists, who like to stand in two hemispheres at the same time.

The point of this story, however, is to tell about the sign in the pond. No good park is complete without a pond, and Greenwich Park has a very nice pond tucked away at its south end. Along with ducks and other birdlife, there are water lilies and the kinds of plants that are found in all the best ponds. There is also a sign in the pond that notifies passersby what they should do if they happen to see someone in distress, floundering in the water. It tells them to go and fetch the life-belt. It doesn't tell them to dive in and try to save the desperate person, but it does, in a general sort of way, identify the location of the life belt. It is *On The West Wall Of The Police Station*, the sign says. It does not, alas, tell you where the police station *is* in the nearly two hundred acres of rolling hills and trees that make up the park, or how far away it lies from the pond; that is up to the brave rescuer to find out.

When the heroic soul has found the police station, he or she must then determine which wall is the *west* one. That should not be too hard; it is the one with the life belt hanging on it. Now, although strange signs are as English as tea rooms, one has to wonder what the park authorities were thinking when they stuck the sign in the pond in the first place. They might at least have given some basic directions, and some idea of how long the round trip would be.

The strange sign in the pond

Then, after telling the drowning victim, "Hang on there!" the rescuer could say, "I'll be back with a life belt in twenty minutes." At least the drowning victim would then know where he, or she, stood—or floated. With the would-be rescuer setting off without a clue to search the four corners of the park, the chances of survival for the poor victim would be less than auspicious. Even if the rescuer found the police station and retrieved the life belt from the west side, it would still be an awfully cumbersome thing to be carrying at a dead sprint.

I doubt if the life belt has ever been used, it does not seem at all practical; by the time the life belt is brought back to the pond, it will probably be too late for the gasping soul in the water. Still, as they say, it is the thought that counts.

WHERE WE ARE NOW: ENDINGS

EAR PLYMOUTH, IN MASSACHUSETTS, between Long Pond and Round Pond, sits a magical camp set among the pine woods of the Miles Standish Forest. During the summer months it is filled with dancers and music makers brought together by the Country Dance and Song Society of America. When you first find it, you may think you have stumbled upon Brigadoon. The camp is called Pinewoods.

I have been going to it for more than fifty years and have made many friends, learned songs and dances, and plan on making more visits while I am able to do so. For years I went by myself, but now I go with my wife Louise, a wonderful dancer and storyteller. Friends who know us both often refer to her as Saint Louise. I am not sure why.

About forty years ago, in the 1970s, one of the invited guests to Folk Music Week was a elderly, gray-haired man from North Carolina. He had been invited to teach the campers the art of shape note singing, a style of singing the spiritual music embedded in the culture of Appalachia. It is called "shape note singing" because the notes in the song book are represented by squares, ovals, triangles, and so on. The shape indicates where the note is in the scale. These hymns are usually sung in four-part harmony, with the soprano, alto, tenor, and bass sections lined up in an inward-facing square.

The name of the invited guest was Richard Moss, a master singer and leader of shape note singing in churches in Appalachia. In spite of his age, his voice was clear and true, and it carried beautifully through the trees and across the ponds to echo throughout Pinewoods Camp. In addition to the shape notes, he gave all of us a very special song that has stayed with many over the years. I have been singing "Time Has Made a Change" ever since I heard him sing it:

Time has made a change in the old home place,
Time has made a change in each smiling face,
And I know my friends can plainly see
Time has made a change in me.

The changes that come with aging are hard to accept. One gets older but no wiser, and as we slow down, we shrink, and often spend half of the night getting up to go to the bathroom. That is just the way it is for those who reach what some call "The Golden Years." There is nothing golden about them at all. What doesn't hurt doesn't work, and that covers a lot of bits and pieces. Fortunately, in some cases, it is possible to get replacement parts—or parts that will make other parts work better.

I have a condition know as bradycardia, a fancy name for a slow heart beat. This used to be thought of as a good thing if you were a long-distance runner, but it had been giving me some problems. I went to a cardiologist to see what he thought. He told me that I needed a pacemaker and showed me one he had in his pocket. It is about the size of a silver dollar with two attached electrical wires, and it is filled with the most incredible computerized equipment.

I told him that I would like to have a pacemaker. "OK," he said, "let's do it tomorrow morning."

That is what we did. To install it, the doctor (I suppose I should call him a surgeon) made a small slit up by my right shoulder and then planted the amazing gadget under my skin (I hope it wasn't the one that he had kept in his pocket). Somehow, he connected the electrical wires to my heart. I can't imagine how he did that, but the great thing is, the pacemaker works. At least it has up to now.

Before having the pacemaker, I was having difficulty walking up hills; now, I am almost ready for the New York City Marathon—not right away, mind you, but sometime down the road. A friend of mine in south east London took up the pole vault at the age of seventy-five, enters competitions for his age group, and often wins. Maybe being the only entrant helps, but it is still inspirational.

Today, I live with Louise in a small town called Leonia, in North East New Jersey, right next to the Big Apple (as New York City is often called). Leonia is a wonderful town, and its citizenry has a reputation for fierce independence. I have lived there for the past forty years, so by now I am really a Leonian, but I still miss much about life in Old England—London, old friends, beer at room temperature—and though I have only spent a third of my life in England, I still remain at heart a South East Londoner.

You can always tell a Londoner, but you can't tell him much.

About the Author

David Jones is an English transplant. In 1965, he came to New York State on a six-month contract to work as an engineer. One thing led to another, and now, more than fifty years later, he is still in the U.S.A. He lives with his wife Louise in New Jersey, fondly referred to as "The Garden State." Over these years he has combined engineering with acting and being a singer of traditional folksong, much of which is sung a cappella. His singing, especially of songs from the great days of sail, has led to travels in Europe and Australia, and to many venues throughout the States. He has made a number of recordings, which, along with theater performances, have been kindly reviewed.